Assignment: Spy

Oluf Reed Olsen

(abridged from *Two Eggs on My Plate*)

SBS SCHOLASTIC BOOK SERVICES
New York Toronto London Auckland Sydney

Previously published in the United States and British Empire under the title: TWO EGGS ON MY PLATE. Copyright 1952 by George Allen & Unwin, Ltd., London. American edition edited and published by Rand McNally & Company. Copyright 1953 by George Allen & Unwin, Ltd. This abridged edition is published by Scholastic Book Services, a division of Scholastic Magazines, Inc., by arrangement with Rand McNally & Company, and is for sale in the United States and Canada only, and is not to be imported into other countries of the British Empire.

4th printing, November 1968

Printed in the U.S.A.

CONTENTS

To

Carl Sigurd Elligers

Assignment: Spy

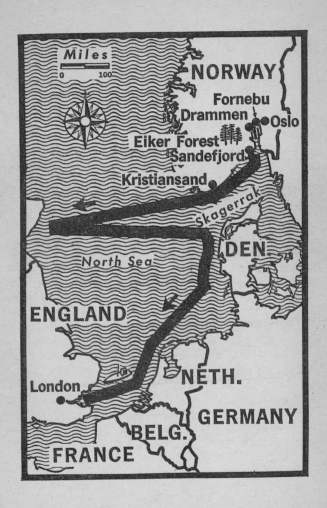

1 April 1940

THIS STORY BEGINS soon after April 9, 1940. The German invasion of Norway was in full swing, with Oslo, Kristiansand, Stavanger, Bergen, and Trondheim occupied by the enemy. Fighting was still going on in the interior of the country, but most of Norway's people were still paralyzed with amazement at what was happening outside their very door.

After the Nazis had overrun and conquered Poland, the war on the Western Front had settled down to what newspapers and diplomats sneeringly called the "sitzkrieg." For eight months the "phony war" continued, with its strange period of inactivity. Then, suddenly, things began to happen. A British destroyer entered Norwegian territorial waters to rescue several hundred British merchant seamen from the German prison ship *Altmark,* and on April 7 England began laying mines inside the Norwegian three-mile limit.

Then, at dawn on April 9, the German war machine struck at Denmark and Norway with all the fury of the Polish campaign. By mid-afternoon all Denmark had been occupied and the government had capitulated.

From then on, Denmark was a handy springboard to Norway, where most of the fighting was to take place in this phase of the war.

Most Norwegians didn't know until after the Nazi invasion that our government and population had been sown with German agents and Norwegian traitors; or that for weeks, merchant ships had been entering the ports of Norway, their holds crowded with German soldiers.

Like most of my countrymen, at first I was completely bewildered, and, as a lad of twenty-one with no previous military training, I did not understand the seriousness or full significance of what was taking place. Still, I was filled with a sense of outrage, with a fierce desire to fight back against the invader. And I was not alone. With a good friend of mine, Kaare Moe from Bestum, a suburb of Oslo, I tried to get a clearer idea of what we ought to do, and where we could report for duty once our course was clear.

The morning of the ninth, at the East Station, we approached a cadet officer in the Army, but his reply was the same one that hundreds of patriotic Norwegians had been given: "Just go home, resistance is useless!"

Such a rebuff from a military officer had undoubtedly been influenced by enemy instructions, and the same evening we laid our plans for a long trip northward. These plans were not carried out, however, for other friends gave us an account of conditions at Hvalsmoen, where we had thought of reporting.

The whole region was being bombed by the Germans, and evidently confusion prevailed there just as it did in the far south of Norway. Moreover, we came in contact with a British captain working for the secret British intelligence system in Oslo. He urged us to abandon our plans for a journey to northern Norway through Sweden, and to report for service with him instead.

Our first assignments were small and seemingly insignificant ones, yet our greatest wish was being fulfilled—we were doing our duty as Norwegians.

We were put to work photographing, sketching, and mapping German airfields, defense works, and military positions and installations; also, finding out all we could about German troop movements: what kind of troops were concerned, to what units the troops which passed through Oslo belonged, where they came from, and where they were going.

This was work which often led to exciting minor incidents which suited our then fairly modest demands. But at that time our activities were inspired to some extent by a thirst for adventure; the whole business was a manifestation of sporting enthusiasm.

It was while fighting was going on a little way outside Oslo that we were given our first sabotage job. Small parties of Norwegian volunteers were fighting a hard battle against German motorized detachments; the enemy was far superior in both numbers and equipment.

One of these volunteer parties sent out a runner on skis through the German positions. He arrived early one morning with the following information: the

Norwegian forces about Skaret (about twenty miles
from Oslo) and the road along the Tyrifjord could not
hold out much longer. Supplies for the German forces
along the roads from Oslo, and along the Drammen
Road via Lysaker and Sandvika, must be cut off at any
cost so that the Norwegian troops could prepare fresh
positions to the north.

Four bridges were to be blown up—one on the road
from Drammen to Hönefoss via Skaret, both bridges at
Sandvika, and the bridge over the Lysaker River at
Lysaker. All were to be blown up at exactly four
o'clock the next morning, so there was not much time.
The Lysaker bridge was our job.

Neither Kaare nor I had the least idea of how a
bridge should be blown up, although we had handled
dynamite before when clearing the ground where our
Scout hut stood. We knew how a charge was fired
with fuse, percussion cap, and ordinary dynamite,
but that was a far cry from blowing up a bridge. How
much dynamite was needed and how should it be
placed? Clearly we were not qualified for the task.
But there was no time for talking; the job had to be
done, whether we got others to carry out the actual
blasting or did the best we could ourselves.

As it was, we knew no one else who could be enlisted
for the job in so short a time. It was up to us to blow
up the bridge, and our plans were laid accordingly. I
had a stock of dynamite, stolen two days before from
different establishments in the neighborhood, with the
object of making hand grenades.

We needed a third man, however, and it was not

hard to find people who would be glad to have a hand in it. The difficulty was to find a man who could hold his tongue, who could control the desire which, especially in those days, was a common failing of practically the entire Norwegian population—the desire to make oneself popular through taking part in some exciting escapade, and telling about it.

There was another factor, too, to be considered. Among the friends we consorted with daily, nearly all were eager to join the fight in progress. Discussion and fantastic plans were first on the daily program. The greatest mistake here was that every action was planned on private initiative, which could as easily hurt our own side as the Germans: often, indeed; that was more likely. We therefore made it our guiding principle from the very beginning that no one but ourselves should know that we were working for a particular organization, regardless of how many helpers we were obliged to recruit for the various tasks.

Kaare's brother Leif became our third man for this special job. The afternoon was used for a short reconnaissance of Lysaker bridge and its surroundings. The bridge was probably being watched, but no regular sentry was to be seen. For ten minutes we stood hanging over the parapet, while motorized equipment passed over the bridge in long convoys. To our great disappointment we perceived that the middle pier, which we had thought of "moving" a bit, was enclosed in timber from below the surface of the water up to the top, where the three main beams of the bridge rested.

This was a serious setback to our plans, for obviously we could not begin to strip off a board covering in the middle of the night to reach the most effective places between the large stones of which the pier was built. It would make too much noise.

Round the pier of the bridge, however, down close to the water's edge, there was a wide projection, probably intended for reinforcement. By means of a ladder about twelve feet long, let down on a rope and leaning against the pier itself, it would be possible to get down under the bridge in a matter of seconds. From that point, the possibility of blowing it up effectively could be investigated more closely.

The evening was spent in further preparations. The dynamite was packed in four separate parcels, sixteen pounds in each; each parcel was fitted with a double fuse twenty feet long and a powerful charge with two percussion caps on the end of each fuse. A twenty-foot fuse would give us about a quarter of an hour to get away, according to the calculations we had made with the material we had in stock—if everything went as planned.

At one o'clock that morning a rather curious silent procession made its way toward Lysaker bridge: Leif with a light ten-foot ladder over his shoulder, Kaare with a pack containing thirty-four pounds of dynamite, and myself with a similar parcel containing dynamite, fuses, and percussion caps.

There were not many people out so late, but every time we heard someone approaching we flung ourselves into the ditch for a few minutes and lay motionless until he had passed.

About a hundred yards from the bridge we stopped, took off our loads, and went on under cover of some bushes and trees. Some fifteen yards from our goal we lay still, watching the outline of the bridge. Now and then a German car passed, but otherwise the neighborhood seemed deserted.

We lay there for a good half-hour. Then the now familiar sound of iron-tipped boots rang through the silence of the night. The steps came from the Drammen Road itself, from Oslo toward the bridge. We lay as silent as mice, staring till our eyes nearly left their sockets, and listened.

The light shone on two helmets—two German sentries stood out in silhouette against the night sky as they passed over the bridge. I stole cautiously after them in rubber shoes, only to discover in the next five minutes that the Germans had a larger area to patrol than the immediate neighborhood of the bridge—they went on up through Lysaker itself.

Minutes passed while we lay waiting for the sentries to come back, so that we could roughly time their round and get an idea of how long the intervals would be in which we could work undetected.

The plan of procedure was repeated in whispers for the last time: every man knew exactly what was to happen—and exactly what a mistake would mean both for our task and for himself. The bridge must be blown up at all costs. Leif's task was to keep a lookout from a place fixed in advance, while Kaare and I did the work under the bridge. If the sentries discovered anything while we were setting the charge, it would be up to Leif to warn us. At sixteen minutes to four Leif was to leave his post and go home as quickly as he could by a roundabout route.

Time passed. The sentries crossed the bridge; five minutes past three! Forty minutes to do it in! A pressure of Leif's hand, a last checkup of the revolvers, and Kaare and I crept noiselessly toward the bridge with the dynamite on our backs and the ladder between us. At that moment the sound of a car engine broke the silence and forced us to lie flat in the ditch for a few seconds. A German truck passed with troops on board, then the road was clear again. We reached the middle of the bridge, lowered the ladder cautiously over the parapet, and made fast the rope which held it. Kaare climbed over and down onto the pier of the bridge; I followed, and the rope was jerked loose from the parapet. We stood side by side under the bridge and listened—all was still.

Kaare chose that critical moment to whisper a joke in my ear. "Shut up!" I whispered back, "or I'll set a match to the dynamite when you've got it!" Even though it was too dark to see, I knew Kaare was smiling mischievously. In the months that followed, I was to learn that Kaare's special sense of humor always came to the fore at just such moments.

We continued our preparations in silence. The ladder was moved under the bridge and set up against the center of the pier. Kaare held it while I climbed

up to find the best places for the charges. It soon became clear that it was impossible to use four different
places. Instead of blowing the whole pier to bits, as
we had originally planned, we would have to content
ourselves with shattering the roadway and doing as
much other damage as possible.

Our reflections were suddenly interrupted by footsteps. It could only be the two German sentries. We
remained motionless. Kaare hung onto the ladder with
both hands while I clung to the top of it. Two pairs of
iron-tipped boots resounded on the road above us,
grew louder—and died away again.

We had only twenty minutes left when something
happened which almost took our breath away. A car
came from the Lysaker side, drew near, and stopped
in the middle of the bridge right over our heads!
Orders and loud talk reached us, standing on tenter-
hooks below. I felt a slight trembling of the ladder,
perhaps from my own trembling legs, perhaps from
Kaare's convulsive grip. The vehicle on the bridge was
a German car!

We did not understand all that was said, but this
much was clear: someone had been discovered trying
to blow up the Sandvika bridges farther out along the
Drammen Road, and now orders had been given to
reinforce the guard at the Lysaker bridge by two men!
An extra close watch must be kept!

The car started again and disappeared in the direction of Oslo.

Now there were four men on the bridge. They talked
together in low voices as they went over toward one

parapet. For a few breathless seconds they stood discussing the possibility of the bridge's being effectively blown up; then they moved on again, and this time their steps died away toward Lysaker. From the looks of things, they did not take their task too seriously, nor the attempt to blow up the Sandvika bridges. But what were their plans?

I glanced at the illuminated face of my wrist watch: a quarter to four! The sweat ran down me as I worked feverishly; the whole charge under the central beam, the fuse down—and I after it. We had not a second to lose: the Germans might be back at any moment! An old raincoat served as a screen while I lighted the fuses.

Meanwhile Kaare had set up the ladder against the outside of the pier, and it took him a fraction of a second to clamber up, stick his head over the edge, and report that all was clear. A moment later we were both on the bridge. We left the ladder where it was and made off as quckly as we could up toward the Vekkerö Road. For the first hundred yards we went cautiously, and silently. After that the only consideration was speed.

Fourteen minutes later we stopped, panting, and listened expectantly. Not a sound! Fifteen minutes—still as quiet as the grave! Kaare turned quickly to me and said: "You don't think we've got to do it again?"

Before I could open my mouth to reply, the roar from Lysaker shattered the air. One handshake, and

Kaare disappeared up toward the Baerum Road, I homeward, toward Montebello.

Next morning, we were the anonymous subjects of an excited attack in the Oslo radio news bulletin. Vidkun Quisling—whose name has become a synonym for "traitor" but who in those days was the pillar of the law, peace, and order—made a speech of "admonition" to the Norwegian people. He said among other things that during the night there had been one regrettable case of sabotage and attempts at sabotage elsewhere. Fortunately these attempts had been foiled and the malefactors taken into custody by the German police. However, a bridge in the Oslo area had been partly destroyed, but the police were hot on the trail and expected to make an arrest in the course of the day.

At nine o'clock the telephone rang. It was Kaare. Had I heard the fearful explosion in the night and did I know that someone had tried to blow up the Lysaker bridge?

No, I hadn't heard anything—I was such a sound sleeper.

Yes, his brother Leif had just heard about it from another friend who had gone down and had a look at the bridge, so there must be something to the report.

At ten o'clock I was up at Kaare's, and with Leif we joined the many inquisitive Sunday walkers who had collected around Lysaker. The bridge itself was closed to traffic, but unfortunately, as far as we could see it had not been completely destroyed. Still, the damage

was sufficient to stop the transport scheduled to leave
Oslo the same morning with reinforcements for the
troops engaged in the country near Skaret-Hönefoss,
and to delay it for a day and a half, thus reducing the
pressure on our Norwegian troops in those parts.

How the police had got on the trail of the saboteurs,
as Quisling reported, remained for the present an un-
solved mystery to us and to the other walkers. Their
house-to-house searches, which were still going on
while we were looking at the bridge, were fruitless;
so were a number of random arrests. As far as we were
concerned, our only regret was that the plan had not
been carried out in its entirety, as the breaking of a
single link was thus rendered less valuable.

On Sunday afternoon, when we reported to the
"captain," we learned of the German threat to shoot
twenty Norwegians as a reprisal for what had happened. But happily the threat was not carried out.

Not long after the Lysaker bridge episode, the German High Command took over the few antiaircraft
positions the Norwegian army had had around Oslo,
and developed them on a large scale. Among these
positions was Björnebo, a suburb about two miles
west of Oslo. The most modern antiaircraft guns and
heavy machine guns, listening apparatus, and searchlights now replaced our old antiaircraft machine guns.
Björnebo now became, in the earliest days of the occupation, the strongest antiaircraft battery near Oslo,
and it took on great importance during the British
bombing attacks on Fornebu Airfield that summer.

After a short time, a new type of German heavy

machine gun was brought into action at Björnebo, and
we were asked one day if we could obtain detailed
information about it, complete with photographs or
sketches.

British bombers for three nights had plastered
Fornebu Airfield with good results, and the German
crews of the various batteries in the inner Oslofjord
had had a pretty hard time. The gun positions at
Björnebo in those days had no barbed-wire obstacles
of any size, so a Norwegian civilian could get quite
near the guns in daytime. The heavy machine gun in
question had been placed a little way from the main
battery, and stood alone on a small hillock.

After a close reconnaissance of the place, I went up
to the gun one day when all but two of the guards
had gone down to the camp for dinner. When I came
loafing up to the position, one of the guards was busy
greasing the machine gun, while the other was en-
ergetically packing ammunition boxes and evidently
getting everything set up for the next night's bombing
from the British Royal Air Force.

I sauntered up to the gun an indifferently as I
could, saluted the guard, and opened a conversation
by asking for a match. At the same time I offered the
German a cigarette. He was a man of about thirty,
small and thickset with rough hands, presumably a
peasant or workman. At first he seemed little inclined
to talk, but once he had lighted the cigarette his
tongue began to wag.

We talked first about the weather; I told him that
I was a land worker, that my sympathies were entirely

pro-German, that I hated the English and was tremendously impressed by the invincible Nazi war machine. He talked about himself, his wife and three children on a small farm outside Bremen, his faith in Adolf Hitler and the coming New Order in Europe.

After a while I sat down beside the gun. He cleaned, greased, and chatted, and I looked on, now and then interjecting some appropriate remark. We had been using the intimate second-person singular for a long time, and after a bare half-hour we were talking like old school friends. The conversation gradually shifted to some unflattering observations on our common enemy, the English tyrants, then to the bombing raids of the last three days, and now I had the chance of getting in a few remarks about the working of "the fantastic German air defense with its magnificent guns!"

"But how in the world can a machine gun like that fire with such tremendous velocity?" I put the question with blind admiration, and it was with pride that the guard described and showed me every single detail—working, measurements, and improvements effected on his wonderful weapon.

Repeatedly during the demonstration I raised my hat and rubbed my forehead with the back of my hand, coughed, and put my hat on again. Inside the hat, fixed firmly in the lining, was a small camera: a strip of film focused at six feet six inches, a little adapter for longer distances, an automatic winder, and the lens just visible through a small hole in the crown of the hat. The coughing coincided with the taking of

each photograph, to prevent the proud demonstrator
of the machine gun's mechanism from hearing suspicious noises.

I now had an exact description and a series of
splendid photographs of the heavy machine gun under
discussion, thanks to a chance German private. We
parted eternal friends, with a cordial *"auf Wieder-
sehen";* and with a German cigarette in the corner of
my mouth and trying to suppress my elation, I sauntered home to write my report and develop the
photographs.

2   A Visit to Fornebu Airfield

NOT ALL OUR TASKS could be executed as simply and painlessly as the machine-gun assignment.

One night early in July, Kaare Moe and I were lying on our stomachs in a patch of wood at the edge of the northwestern corner of Fornebu Airfield. At that time it was surrounded by a fence nearly ten feet high, with four rows of barbed wire on top. At regular intervals along this fence hung placards: "Photographing most strictly forbidden!" Sentries patrolling the fence that encircled the airfield made it difficult to get in, but it was still relatively easy to take general views from outside.

The task which was to be carried out that night was, in short, to photograph the site of the ammunition and bomb dump, and sketch it with explanatory details. The plan was to be executed as follows: Almost every night British planes bombed the airfield, and, we had learned by reconnaissance, most of the German sentries and all the other personnel deserted their posts and sought safety in the air-raid shelters for the duration of the attack, allowing free access to anyone who could get over or under the fence.

There was just one small detail which might deter any normal person—the bombs dropped by the British planes! But that was a chance which had to be taken. Our plan was to get under the fence and as close to the bomb and ammunition dump as possible, find a suitable place to lie till daylight came, make our sketches, take the photographs, and then get out as best we could.

Our operation would have to begin at exactly the same moment as the British bombing.

For the last time we went through every detail in whispers. But each time the German sentry passed we lay quite still, noting the time he took to make his round. It averaged eight minutes, and that would give us about five minutes in which to do our work, once daylight came.

At seven minutes to twelve the raid warning was sounded. From where we lay we could hear high-pitched orders at the hangars, while the shadows of two sentries hurriedly disappeared along the fence toward the shelters a little way off in the wood. At the same moment there came from the northwest the drone of bombers growing steadily louder.

The moment for action was near. The antiaircraft defenses had long ago opened their deafening concert; heavy antiaircraft guns and heavy and light machine guns in a few seconds transformed the clear, starry night sky into a sparkling fireworks display; where we lay, the ground literally trembled. The planes were now almost overhead; then down came the first parachute flares. Next moment the whole airfield was flooded with light.

An ear-splitting crash; we were flung head over heels. Another—and yet another! The earth trembled and shook beneath us, and earth and stones began to rain down upon us where we lay under some bushes with our hands over our heads.

The first attack was over, and judging by the sound, the planes were now turning toward Oslo. The moment had come!

Two Junker 52's had caught fire close to the longest runway, and a few Germans were already on their way to try to put the fire out.

"Now!"

We made at top speed for the previously chosen point in the fence. A ditch had been dug from the ammunition dump through a light copse which concealed it, over an open space and out under the fence. The ditch was full of water, and our cameras barely escaped a wetting when with a splash we finished up in the ditch side by side.

We were under cover now, and from this point our course of action was relatively simple. It did not take us long to cut through the barbed wire in the ditch under the fence, even allowing time for exploring to make sure there was no alarm system. Once through the hole, we put the wire back as best we could, and went on along the ditch toward the ammunition dump, half-creeping, half-walking.

Meanwhile the bombers had come around again for a new attack. To judge from the sound, there were four of them. They had now evidently changed their tactics, for one plane, presumably the one that had dropped its bombs first, had gone up to a good height, and deliberately flown into the light from one of twenty searchlights in operation.

Anything and everything that could shoot went into action, and the noise was ear-splitting. But the bomber obviously was not troubled; it suddenly made a turn to starboard and was gone. The searchlights worked feverishly, till suddenly a light flashing a series of V's could be seen against the black night sky a little way off. Again all the searchlights were turned on the one plane, and the wild firing continued.

All this time we squatted, watching the lavish spectacle. Then suddenly there was a terrific crash; plane, searchlights, guns, all were blotted out, drowned by a furious ringing and roaring inside my head. I felt myself flung against something—then everything went black.

I cannot say for sure whether I was unconscious for seconds or minutes. I regained consciousness with a curious feeling that something wet was running steadily down my face. Cautiously I opened my eyes. I was lying with my head half under water at the bottom of the ditch, and something heavy and wet lay halfway across me. I thought at first that I was dreaming, and shut my eyes to get back to reality. But no, this was no dream! The heavy wet object which lay across me in a twisted posture began to stir: it was Kaare.

"The devils!" were the first words he spat from his

mouth, along with earth and stones. "If they must drop bombs just where we're doing a job, they don't have to aim at us!"

I agreed entirely; but I was too busy feeling to see whether I was still intact, and the camera dry, to be able to give an acceptable answer.

We stuck our heads cautiously over the edge of the ditch. There, barely twenty-five yards from where we lay, and about forty yards from the ammunition dump, were six gaping craters stretching more or less in a straight line over toward the hangars!

We had now come so close to the ammunition dump that, according to our prearranged plan, we were to separate. One of us was to remain in the ditch to take photographs of the dump which would clearly show its position in relation to the larger part of the airfield. The other was to try to reach a point southwest of the dump to take photographs of it at 315^0 true north, so that the position of the dump in relation to the central building and the hangars would be clearly shown.

In this way cross bearings on the ammunition dump would be obtained, and it could subsequently be pinpointed on the map. We had tossed a coin to decide who should carry out the last part of the task, which was undoubtedly the worst since the distance back was nearly twice as far. The hazardous job had fallen to Kaare.

Our watches were synchronized now for the last time: a handshake, a glance over the edge to see if all was clear, and Kaare vanished into the darkness. The luminous dial of my wrist watch showed four minutes past one.

Hardly three minutes after Kaare had disappeared the British bombers came in for a new attack. This time I settled myself flat against the edge of the ditch with both arms over my head and my jacket pulled well up. There were four more deafening crashes, but this time not nearly so loud as in the previous attack. Almost at the same time came a series of lesser reports, and when, after a moment to steady my nerves, I peeped cautiously over the edge of the ditch, I could not help exclaiming, "Good Work!"

If no one else heard it, it was nevertheless an expression of silent admiration for the crews of the planes high up in the night sky. The four bombs had made hits right across the longest runway and, better still, a stick of incendiary bombs had set fire to a whole row of planes in the northern corner of the airfield! It was bright as daylight over there, and yelling Germans were trying frantically to put the fires out. A brilliant spectacle—so brilliant that for a few minutes I completely forgot our own rather dangerous position.

This was the last attack that night. The antiaircraft fire died away, and the planes disappeared in a south-westerly direction. The minutes crept away, and all was relatively quiet again. Only shouted orders and loud curses from the Germans putting out the fires, and occasional explosions from the burning planes, reached the spot where I lay. The sentry guarding the

fence had resumed his patrol, and about every eighth
minute he passed the hole we had made in the fence
wire.

The first hour went quickly enough; so long as the
planes were burning there was entertainment. I was
pretty wet from the rough treatment we had received
during the attack, and my legs, which had to be under
water all the time, had gone to sleep long before. Now
that the excitement was over, the minutes crept past.
I had to stop looking at my watch; it seemed to want
oiling badly—I had never thought a watch hand could
move so slowly. I began instead to calculate the time
by the regular passing of the sentry. At last he too
seemed to have fallen asleep, and I thought for a
moment of following his example.

It was nearly three, and the sky in the east had long
ago begun to assume a rather lighter hue; day was
about to break. But it was chilly, and I was horribly
cold. For the hundredth-and-I-don't-know-how-many
times, I pulled my sleeve up a little and looked at my
watch. Five past three! Still fifty-five minutes to wait
before we could go into action!

The sentry had just passed the hole, and as usual I
raised myself high enough above the edge of the ditch
to look around and see that all was in order. I remained
motionless and held my breath! Two tractors with
bomb trailers behind them, carrying nine men in all,
came driving toward the ammunition dump! I hardly
dared breathe; cold and numbed feet were forgotten
in a second. Which entrance would they use? The
south, where Kaare lay, or the north, where I lay?

Yard by yard they approached the fork where the road divided to go to the two entrances. North! When the first tractor swung toward me, I sank back into the ditch, pulling the fresh leafy twigs we had brought for camouflage well over my head. The tractors passed within four yards of the spot where I lay. The conversation between the four men on one tractor and the five on the other could be heard plainly; they were talking about the night's bombing.

It was with some relief that I heard them stop in front of the entrance to the ammunition dump. So far everything had gone well. But this was something we had overlooked in our otherwise meticulous plans—that planes should be loaded up with bombs so soon after the night's attack.

How long would the Germans stay in the dump? Would all nine leave as soon as they had done the necessary loading up, or was this only the start of a prolonged spell of work? Had Kaare seen them come, and had he counted them so that when his photographing was finished he could, as arranged, return to the ditch where I lay without being detected by some straggler?

A string of questions raced through my brain, but only time would answer them. I lay listening, still motionless. The northern entrance to the ammunition dump was just opposite, and the slightest movement would be enough to betray me. If earlier minutes had seemed like hours, seconds now seemed even longer. I lay with my arm in front of me so that I could follow the minute hand on my watch dial.

A quarter past three—half-past three—twenty-five minutes to four—twenty minutes to four—eighteen minutes to four, and then! First one tractor, and close behind it the other, came slowly toward me. Past! I lifted my head inch by inch, my eyes fixed on the northern descent to the ammunition dump. Not a soul to be seen!

Just as carefully I again raised my head, covered with foliage, just above the edge of the ditch. One—two—three—yes, nine Germans in all were on the two tractors disappearing with their cargoes of explosives toward the upper part of the airfield.

The way was now clear for the time being—only the regular passing of the sentry demanded attention. It was now very nearly four o'clock. Day had come, and in the east the sky was flaming red. Fires were still burning among the planes over by the runway, and dense smoke still poured up.

Six minutes to four; the sentry passed for the last time before being relieved. The moment for action had come at last. I rose cautiously and examined my surroundings with care. There was not a German to be seen nearer than the hangars, only the back of the sentry who was slowly moving off and disappearing behind some trees.

One—two—three photographs, all with different exposures to get as good results as possible. Then I crawled on my stomach over the edge of the ditch into the grass, my compass in one hand the camera in the other. I was to take a few photographs of the dump at 225° true north, just as I had done with the greater part of the southwestern section of the airfield. Fortunately, the direction coincided with a big raspberry bush, in the shelter of which the remaining photographs were taken.

Back on my stomach to the ditch, and this part of the job was completed without misadventure as far as I was concerned. It was now three minutes past four. I cautiously assumed my previous position, with leaves and twigs over my head, and did some sketching.

But how was Kaare getting on? It had been agreed that he should take photographs at the same time, assuming the coast was clear, and then wait twenty minutes at the spot where he was lying. We calculated that the new sentry who began his patrol a little after four would keep a specially sharp lookout on his first two rounds, and then slack off a bit after having seen nothing suspicious within his area.

I lay still and looked at my watch. The sentry came and passed. Exactly seven minutes past four. I followed the minute hand, anxious to see how long he was taking. Nine minutes—there he came again, and passed. Sixteen minutes past four. Four minutes more, and Kaare would begin to crawl. Twenty past four! Kaare had started on his difficult journey back to the ditch.

The sentry passed again; this time he had taken ten minutes. Good fellow, the new sentry! Again he passed, this time on his way toward the place where Kaare was toiling up to the ditch. Tense minutes followed, and I strained my ears to listen. Suddenly a cracking noise broke the silence—a sound like the breaking of a dry twig. It came from the direction in which Kaare should now be.

I grew hot with anxiety. The sentry should have passed long ago on his upward journey; a quarter of an hour had gone since he last came by. Had he heard what I heard, become suspicious, and gone into the scrub to investigate? I was just getting ready to raise myself up for a closer look, when the heavy dragging step of a sleepy sentry broke the silence. Thank God— not this time!

The sentry passed. Four minutes later Kaare slid cautiously down the side of the ditch smiling broadly but as black as a sweep! A silent pressure of the hand, and we both sank down motionless, with the foliage over our heads. The sentry passed again; and now for the way out under the fence. About ten minutes to do it in. Cautiously, on hands and knees, we moved along in the ditch; the barbed wire was pushed aside, we scrambled through and replaced the barbed wire as far as possible. Then on in the ditch across the open area and into the woods we scurried.

After nine minutes we stopped. The sentry must not hear anything suspicious now that the worst of the job was over. We waited five minutes, and then continued into thicker wood and across the main road into Oslo, where our bicycles were hidden. There I heard Kaare's story of his hours of waiting and the journey back on his stomach.

It was in the last stage that things had nearly gone wrong. Without noticing it Kaare had laid his arm on a dry twig, which snapped when the sentry was

on his way down and close by. The man had undoubtedly heard the noise, for he had stopped and
stood for a few seconds staring in through the fence.
Then, hearing nothing more to arouse his suspicions,
he had continued on his round. And we had success-
fully completed another mission.

3 We're on Our Way to England

EARLIER IN THIS STORY I touched upon the great importance of holding our tongues, the constant danger that loose tongues could cost Norwegian lives. Yet my generation, in April, 1940, and the days that followed, had difficulty in understanding the vital need for completely obeying this paragraph in the orders of the day. Of course, talking too freely was not exclusively a Norwegian weakness the first year of the war, and we at least had the excuse that we were unaccustomed to wartime restrictions, there having been no war in our country for about 125 years.

Nevertheless, loquacity was our great difficulty, even in the earliest days when intelligence work and espionage were relatively simple matters by later standards. It was hard to enlist fellow workers who could resist the temptation to tell their friends and relatives what they were doing. This was why, in the summer of 1940, as the result of a series of unhealthy incidents, Kaare Moe and I had to flee Oslo and escape to parts where we were not known.

On one of these trips we paid a short visit to Gardermoen Airfield with orders to get photographs of the airfield itself, along with the hangars, repair shop, and ammunition dump, Gardermoen, which is about twenty miles north of Oslo, had before the invasion been used by the Norwegian Army as a training ground, and parts of it as a reserve airfield.

The training ground and its surroundings were admirably suited for laying out airfields on a large scale; their strategic position for military operations was excellent and so was their geographical position, which made an effective defense possible.

The German guard work at Gardermoen at that time was very bad, and we soon saw that it wasn't even necessary to have "legitimate" work at the airfield to get the photographs. With our cameras inside our shirts, or in some cases built into a toolbox with a hole in the side for the lens and a release string under the handle, we pottered about the airfield in working clothes and took the photographs which were later used in England as a basis for intelligence work and espionage at Gardermoen.

Neither of us, however, derived any real personal satisfaction from the work we were doing. We hadn't had any training for it at all, and the result depended more on luck than on efficient and methodical execution. The important question, therefore, was how long those directing our operations would be able to keep things going without being caught.

The Norwegian Government, which was now established in London along with our King, had ordered all airmen to leave Norway as quickly as possible and join a new Norwegian Air Force being formed in

England and Canada. Many had already succeeded in getting out of Norway by boat across the North Sea to the Shetlands or Scotland, and throughout the fall of 1940 the idea of following their example became more deeply rooted in our minds. And by degrees, as various of our undertakings failed to end as we meant them to, this growing desire to pack up and clear out became a compelling necessity.

We encountered many difficulties. The three things we needed most were a crew, a boat, and equipment— and these three things in themselves were serious problems at that time. The question of a crew gave rise to arguments one would not have thought possible under prevailing conditions. But the fact remained that there were very few indeed of our friends and acquaintances who at that time would even consider leaving all they had, completely breaking with the past, and going over to England to fight.

"The war might be over before one gets there!" was the usual argument. This was unfortunately the tenor among a large part of the male population of Oslo in the autumn of 1940. We still found it hard to understand and realize that the struggle in progress between the great powers of Europe was also a struggle for the existence of our own little country and its people.

In my own case it may then have been as much a longing for adventure as anything, combined with deep-seated, perhaps even subconscious, idealism, that made me put the plan into execution. Kaare Moe was the only one of my friends who really saw things as I did and was willing to risk everything in the great undertaking. He reasoned that even if he was not a commercial pilot as I, and might not have the necessary qualifications to become an airman, he could, with his education and experience, make himself useful in many other ways; there was even a chance that he might be accepted as a pupil at the flying school and get his training in Canada.

Never, either before or later, have I met a man who threw himself into a task so wholeheartedly as Kaare Moe. He meant more to his family, perhaps, than most fellows his age; when still quite young he had had to assume responsibility for them when his father died, and yet he always had time for his friends. No one else I have known was so punctual in the discharge of his duty to his mother and his two brothers, as well as his duty to society.

Kaare Moe was also a Scout, second in command of No. 3 Bestum troop, and the promise he had given with his hand on the flag was always his highest ideal. We had worked together in the Scout movement for some years, and I never met anyone who lived up to this promise in the same degree as Kaare.

The plan for a voyage to Britain, however, was to prove more complicated than we had at first thought. It was no simple matter to obtain a serviceable boat. The Germans had long ago become alive to the increasing traffic from the west coast of Norway over to Britain; fishing boats were always disappearing—and the British radio was reporting the arrival of many refugees from Norway.

This resulted in increased activity on the part of the

German Police. The guards along the coast and in the larger towns of the west and south were strengthened considerably; every boat moving along or outside the skerries was required to have a special permit from the German Harbor Police, and every sale and purchase of a boat of any size had to be sanctioned by the same body.

For the Oslofjord the sailing regulations were somewhat simpler, probably because the Germans could not imagine any Norwegian trying to sail the distance from Oslo to Britain. All traffic in the Oslo basin was unhampered apart from a few military penalties, but no one might sail through or outside the Dröbak Sound without permission from the German Harbor Police in Oslo.

German restrictions on the purchase and sale of boats made it very difficult to get a fishing smack of about forty to fifty feet. We found that people were afraid to sell to strangers; and the few who were willing to sell behind the backs of the German authorities demanded prices far beyond our ability to pay.

We had a pretty good idea of what we wanted for sailing in the skerries, as we had both sailed in comparatively small boats since we were boys. But sailing in the open sea, we were told, was something quite different, and would put our experience to a pretty severe test. The North Sea on a quiet summer day was one thing—the North Sea after the autumn gales was another!

The plan gradually took shape in the late hours of the night. Charts and maps were obtained from various private quarters—they were not for sale in the shops, having been confiscated by the Germans—and our route down the coast was planned. Other necessary equipment for the voyage was collected slowly, bit by bit, from different sources.

But here, too, we met with difficulties. Those whom we let in on our secret, and whose support for the enterprise we had reckoned on absolutely, still went about wearing a faintly skeptical smile. Wherever we applied, we felt that the words "a boyish prank" were whispered behind our backs each time we left. But there were others who, although skeptical as to the result, were willing to help us in spite of the risk involved. Among these was an Oslo dentist, Juell-Nielsen, who, in partnership with a friend, owned the lifeboats *Bergen* and *Stavanger*.

I did not know him personally, but got in touch with him through a friend. We hoped at first to charter or buy one of these boats, and possibly get the dentist to make the trip with us. But we failed to accomplish any of these things. The Germans had for a long time had their eye on the *Stavanger*, which was lying in Oslo, and the dentist's friend had the *Bergen* down at Sandefjord. As for getting the dentist to make the trip, this was out of the question, as his wife was ill and he could not leave his family.

In other ways, however, the dentist was of great help to us. He had sailed across the North Sea himself in summer in a small boat and had done a good deal of sea sailing as a hobby. Consequently he could tell us what we might expect and what precautions to take to come safely through possible bad weather. He also gave us much good advice about equipment, advice which later was invaluable.

One item in the program still remained open—a boat, one that could really stand rough wear. One possibility after another was considered and rejected, till one day we came across an eighteen-foot smack-built half-decker which was for sale. The boat was inspected and accepted one afternoon in the middle of August. Certainly, eighteen feet were nothing to boast about, but as she lay drawn up on the slip she did not look too bad by our standards.

After we had paid for the boat, the owner told us that the bottom dated from 1909, but that he himself had built the three upper strakes and the deck about a year ago; the mast was fairly new and the sails not too bad. The boat had an old Bolinder motor, but this the owner could not guarantee. As far as he knew, it had not been used much in the last ten years!

I got the money for the boat, 1,000 crowns, by selling my motorcycle. To avoid "public control" of the sale, the motorcycle was sold to an elderly engineer in Oslo, a man who had never sat on a motorcycle in his life and in all probability never would. But he was one of the few who in those days had 1,000 crowns in ready money, not under control in a frozen bank account, and like the good Norwegian he was, he put his money into an enterprise in which he would have liked to participate himself.

A few days later the boat was sailed in from the Bundefjord to Bestumkilen, outside Oslo, in a fresh northerly wind—a maiden trip which was enough to raise doubts in our minds as to the result of the "great voyage" and the boat's true qualifications. Any fairly strong gust of wind made the boat heel till her rail was under water.

I sailed and—Kaare bailed! The water simply squirted in through cracks in the new bulwarks. We had plenty of time to think as we sat, and in our thoughts we pictured the same boat in a gale out in the North Sea. "There'll probably be a leak or so in the bulwarks, as she hasn't been sailed for some years," were the seller's last words, and they remained fresh in our memory during the following six weeks.

Kaare and I said little as we went into town. We both hoped that this leaky condition would correct itself when the wood had swelled for a few days; of course there was nothing new about leaks in a boat which had been laid up for a long time. As for her noticeable wetness, a couple of hundred pounds of ballast, in addition to what was in her now, would do wonders. In the meantime, one thing must be said in favor of the seller and his boat: she certainly was a good sailer!

Early next morning I met Kaare down on the quay. "She's a bit lower in the water today than when we left her yesterday!" he said, pointing to our newly acquired treasure. I just nodded. What a sight! When we came alongside the marvelous craft, our nautical spirits sank. The water on board stood a good foot and a half above the cabin floor: mattresses and other gear from the tiny cabin were floating about.

Words were unnecessary, but England at that moment seemed remote and historic! Here something had to be done, and quickly. Every day that passed brought us nearer to autumn and its gales.

The boat was now hauled up onto the slip at Bestumkilen and the state of affairs explained to the owner of the slip, Mr. Skeie, who was an old acquaintance. We hinted that there was a possibility of our starting a new firm, the North Sea Shipping Company. We left the rest to him, and he promised to do his best.

"She'll never be watertight," he said, "the bottom's too rotten and the new upper part with the deck too inaccurately built. These things apart, I should advise most strongly against any participation in the North Sea Shipping Company with this craft!" Those were the boatbuilder's last words.

Apart from all the other difficulties I have mentioned, we had something else to contend with: shortage of time and money. But we must do it, and we would do it!

There was another problem: Would two men be enough on the voyage across? In fine weather, yes; in a gale, in all probability not. But it would be impossible to get hold of a third man. There was only one who was willing, and that was Kaare's brother. Of course he was only a boy of sixteen, but he was still capable of working turn and turn about with us. But cold fact made his coming impossible.

The chances of getting to England across the North Sea in autumn in an "unsuitable" eighteen-foot boat were about even, and that was the answer as far as

Leif was concerned. It would be more than enough if one member of the family took this chance.

While the boat was undergoing a thorough overhauling, we proceeded to one of the last items on the program—getting a sailing permit from the German authorities. For this purpose a series of false papers was produced, papers which showed that we were both employed as travelers by a large wholesale provision firm, whose head office was in Oslo, with branches in Bergen and Trondheim.

As the use of private cars or motorcycles had long ceased and the possibility of travel by land was thus limited, the best solution was the use of a boat—to wit, an eighteen-foot smack-built half-decker with a cabin. By this means we could get into contact along the coast with even the smallest country shop which shared our firm's interests. Provisions were most important to maintaining life, as our German "liberators" of course appreciated.

We now proceeded with the necessary false references to the office of the German naval harbor captain, and after a little conversation the matter was arranged and three special traveling passes and sailing permits issued: Oslo-Mandal, Mandal-Bergen, and Bergen-Trondheim.

Here, in the meantime, an episode occurred which is worth mentioning. During our negotiations with a German clerk with the rank of corporal, we noticed that at 12:30 the entire personnel except the man we were talking to left the room and went down to lunch.

We had been told by the corporal's immediate senior

that when we went into Bergen we should have to go
through a German mine field outside the entrance to
Bergen Harbor. We were advised, therefore, to get
the exact positions of the channel through the mine
field, and the necessity of following these positions
for the sake of our own skins was strongly impressed
upon us.

The corporal now went over to a big filing cabinet
in one corner of the room, pulled out the third drawer
from the top, and took out the first file in the fourth
compartment. With the file in his hand, he went back
to his desk, opened the desk, and took out a photographed chart of South Norway including Trondheim.
With it were two lists of positions for the open channels through the mine fields.

Our eyes nearly popped out of our heads! But at the
same time we let the corporal get a definite impression
that this part of our travel plans did not greatly interest
us; we talked in a low voice about sales prospects for
provisions in the various districts.

The corporal, who sat with his back to us, did not
seem to be interested in anything but getting down to
lunch as quickly as possible. He first looked up the list,
noted five different positions, checked these with the
chart, and then turned to us with a detailed explanation. The conversation was in German, and by now we
had become quite good friends.

We took our leave after having given a satisfactory
answer to the corporal's question as to where he could
find "a good hot Norwegian *Fräulein!*"

Next day we were back at the office of the harbor

captain five minutes before lunch time. There was something about our papers we did not fully understand; would the corporal be so kind as to inquire of his chief? "Yes, with pleasure," said the corporal, and disappeared into the next room.

There was no one else in the room. Like a streak of lightning Kaare was over by the door into the passage and I at the filing cabinet—third drawer from the top, fourth compartment, first file. In an instant the photographed chart and lists were under my shirt, the drawer and cupboard were shut, and I was back at my place outside the barrier!

We were talking about foodstuffs again when the corporal returned a moment later with the answer to our question. One or two inquiries and answers about the "good hot Norwegian girl," and we withdrew.

It was pretty obvious that it would not be long before the half-empty file was discovered, but in all probability it would be longer before the corporal reported the matter, as he would be held responsible for his stupidity. Moreover, so many people, both German and Norwegian civilians, were going in and out of that office every day that certainly suspicion would hardly fall on two innocent commercial travelers. But again the chances were fifty-fifty, and this small but important event was a further stimulus to speedy departure.

The photographed chart proved on closer examination to show in detail the German mine fields laid from the Swedish frontier to Frostahavet, outside Trondheim, from April 8 to August 31, 1940. The two lists showed exactly the open channels for coastal traffic through these mine fields.

I reported for the last time to my English friend the "captain," and asked him if he thought it advisable to take the chart and lists with me on the impending voyage across the North Sea together with our photographs—more than a thousand of them—of German defense works. At his suggestion, the chart and lists were microphotographed at our own photographic workshop in Oslo. The originals were returned to us and placed in a secret chamber on board the boat, while the copies were to be sent to England via Sweden at the first opportunity. Thus one set would get there in any case.

At the same time we received our last orders from the "captain." As many photographs of the German defense works as possible were to be taken on the voyage down the coast. We were to pay special attention to Kristiansand with Kjevik and Mandal Airfields, and find out all we could about the proposed big new airfield at Lista, on the southwest coast of Norway.

Final preparations for the great journey were now continued with increased speed. Our calculations were: fourteen days for the voyage down the coast, at best five days across the North Sea to Scotland, at worst ten days. Food for twenty-four days must be obtained, and this in itself was not a simple matter. Food rationing had been imposed a long time back, and supplies were far from plentiful. But contributions from various private hoards saved the situation for us.

Provisions included a keg of mountain butter—nearly

seven pounds—which my mother procured and which, despite vigorous protests, she insisted on our taking with us. Little did I realize at the time how important this butter would be to us.

I told my mother about the plan a week before we left. I must admit that I had expected strong protests, so her stoicism surprised me. When we were sitting on the veranda at home one afternoon I said:

"A week from today Kaare Moe and I are going to England together to report for duty."

At first my mother did not say a word. She only gave me a penetrating look. Then, slowly: "What clothes do you want me to get ready for you, my boy?"

I shall never forget that afternoon, nor the understanding and support she gave to a plan which might well claim the life she had brought into the world and toiled for through twenty-one long years. She only expressed one wish: She wanted to see the boat in which we were going.

The same evening we three were sitting together in the little cabin on board, and over a cup of good coffee with home-baked cakes we heard her verdict: "A bit small if it came on to blow really hard from the northwest—but with God's help it'll go all right."

This opinion was not to be dismissed lightly. Quite the contrary, for my mother was the daughter of one of Norway's greatest sailing captains, and she herself had seen both the North Sea and the Atlantic in storm and calm.

That evening, August 30, the boat was christened the *Haabet* (Hope). She was named after the last sailing ship my mother's father had sailed across the North Sea from England in the autumn of 1905. That time, too, there were many who considered the voyage sheer madness. The bark *Haabet* leaked like a sieve! But the old skipper was not a man to shrink from adversity and danger, and with his loyal crew he "pumped" the vessel into a Norwegian port through one of the worst storms in the memory of man.

The *Haabet*'s flag accompanied him through three shipwrecks in World War I, hanging as a souvenir in his cabin, and it was always among the few possessions he managed to save. The flag which Kaare and I hoisted a few days later on our *Haabet*'s mast consisted of scraps of my grandfather's old flag sewn together. This time, too, it was to prove that it could bring its crew through safely, though the *Haabet* today lies 150 fathoms deep in the North Sea.

Everything was ready. The boat had been made as watertight as possible. But she still leaked appreciably, and our only chance was that her timbers would swell on the voyage down the coast. We had taken the advice of our friend the dentist and replaced the forehalyard with a new quarter inch wire in case of a gale. In addition to this, the forestay was arranged so that the foresail could also be used as a storm sail in the event an emergency should arise.

A radio receiver was installed on board so that we should be able to keep ourselves informed of any new German ordinances, which at that time were being issued daily. The cabin was fitted with two small bunks, one on each side of a narrow strip down the middle.

It was especially important that we have an adequate supply of fresh water. Two wine kegs holding one and two gallons respectively and a round glass vessel holding three-and-a-quarter gallons were obtained and filled. If worse came to worst and the voyage across took more than ten days, each man would have a ration of two-and-a-half pints a day, which, even allowing for coffee and tea, should be ample.

September 1 opened with a fresh northerly breeze and overcast, just the weather we wanted for the sail from Oslo to Drøbak. Our departure was set for 11:00 A.M. from Bestumkilen, and after a short leave-taking from our respective families Kaare and I went on board. But Friday has always been a bad day to start on, according to an old sailors' superstition, and our own experience seemed to bear this out. The wind died down, and by eleven o'clock it was dead calm with light rain.

Next day the weather had improved. There was a fresh northerly wind and it was fairly clear. A fresh good-by, and this time a real one! On the stroke of eleven we cast off from the buoy and the *Haabet* stood out from Bestumkilen under full sail, running before a fresh breeze. The great voyage had begun.

But the *Haabet* was not the only craft which stood out under full sail from Bestumkilen that morning! Almost at the same time, a racing yacht cast off from

her buoy, and on board her were five German naval
officers. It was not till they came up alongside us that
we realized what kind of company we had, and for a
time we felt uncomfortable. But the Germans did not
appear to have any sinister intentions; all they seemed
to want was a race.

Of course we promptly took up the challenge, and
the two boats sailed along, side by side, southward
down the fjord. At first we led, but the Germans gradually overtook us. All the time a lively conversation
passed between the two crews. Of course, the Germans
were sailing a boat which they had confiscated, a fact
which did not seem to trouble their consciences for a
moment. Their sportsmanlike spirit seemed to reach its
climax when, after having sailed past us twice, they
came up alongside and threw across to us a box containing one cigarette!

Our suspicions of the Germans, however, proved
to be unjustified when, with a bellowed *"auf Wieder-
sehen,"* they altered course 180° and began to cruise
back to Bestumkilen. Soon afterward we, too, altered
course and sailed at full speed toward Dröbak.

What we had been dreaming of for weeks had now
become a reality, and even if this was only the beginning of the great adventure, it was nonetheless a
good start. We were both conscious of the danger
and uncertainty which threw a shadow over the whole
enterprise—not only the actual voyage across the North
Sea, but what the future held for us on the other
side. But at the same time we were too proud to voice
our fears to one another; we were not ready to aban-

don so quickly the enthusiastic illusions we had built up in our own minds in the past months.

At 8:00 P.M. we lay to at Dröbak. Sailing after 9:00 P.M. was forbidden by the Germans, and we had no reason for taking any chances at that time. But in spite of our caution it was not long before we got into difficulties. A half-hour after our arrival, Kaare and I were seated in the little cabin eating our supper, when a German voice hailed us from the wharf. We both started, took a rapid look at what was lying in view, and while Kaare remained below I went up to investigate.

It was a German harbor policeman who wanted to see our papers. I grew hot all over. Had the disappearance of the chart and lists been discovered already? No, I decided, that was not likely, so there was no reason to worry unnecessarily. But evidently something was wrong, for I had the dubious pleasure of spending a good hour and a half at the German harbor office while the policeman responsible checked our papers with Oslo.

It happened, the local policeman told us, that they were looking for a couple of men, but finally he was able to inform us that we were not the men! I breathed a deep sigh of relief when this message came by telephone and I was able to return to the *Haabet*. But that same evening I received another message which neither Kaare nor I understood. We were told that we could not leave Dröbak next day, but must wait for further orders.

Neither of us slept much that first night on board.

We had to make a momentous decision: Whether to take our chance next morning and clear off as soon as it was light, or to await further orders from the Germans. We decided to wait.

Three days passed and we grew tired of waiting. I went up to the German police officers and presented our arguments, based on the agreements which as commercial travelers we had made with our customers southward along the coast. The police rang up Oslo again, and we got permission to proceed instantly without further ceremony.

Fortunately, we had made diligent use of the three days we lay at Dröbak, and we sailed away with a substantial collection of good photographs of the various German defense works in the neighborhood.

The days that followed were unforgettable. Everything went as smoothly as possible, and mile after mile disappeared in our wake; day after day, brilliant weather and a steady fresh breeze. As a rule we kept outside the actual skerries, except when time and our photographic interests demanded a little short cut or detour.

When evening came and the wind died down, we gladly turned into one of the thousand small creeks, cast anchor, and rested. Wherever we went the skerries of South Norway lay open and smiling, islet after islet, rock after rock, clad in the loveliest autumn colors. On some days the sailing was hard, and we had an opportunity of testing the *Haabet's* merits and defects. There were many things which must be put right, many things on board which must be altered and improved.

One day, when we were beating up against a strong southwesterly wind, we got the baptism the *Haabet* needed. We were on a long run southward in the open sea, with close-reefed mainsail and foresail. The wind had been increasing steadily during the day, and the seas were breaking white.

Both Kaare and I were sitting in the open steering cockpit, clad in oilskins from head to foot and dripping wet from the seas which poured in over the deck at regular intervals. A squall literally flung itself over the boat; we heeled over and the water poured in. At the same moment there was a crack like a pistol shot, and the next thing we knew, the close-reefed foresail had torn itself away from the sheet.

The *Haabet* swung up into the wind and rose again half-full of water, while the mainsail and foresail thrashed wildly. The iron shackle between the forestay and the sheet had given way!

Three hours later we were in the shelter of islets and rocks again, richer by an invaluable experience but considerably more skeptical of the *Haabet's* chances on a stormy night in the North Sea. We kept our misgivings to ourselves, however.

The whaling port of Sandefjord had been ruled out before we started from Oslo, because I was too well known among the inhabitants there. We therefore agreed to keep well outside and under no circumstances risk coming into port there. Early one morning we sailed past the entrance and the island of Rauer just outside; it was hazy and bad weather, so we could hardly make out any details, and not a soul was to be seen.

By an odd quirk of fate—and I learned this two years later in Iceland—on that very day our friend the dentist's partner, with the lifeboat *Bergen*, lay waiting for us in Sandefjord Harbor with provisions for three months on board. The dentist had written from Oslo when he first heard of our plans, asking his partner to help us.

The letter had been censored by a man who at that time called himself a good Norwegian, and who took the missive to the addressee in person with a stern warning that letters of that kind ought not to be sent by mail. No reply, therefore, came from Sandefjord. Instead, the dentist's partner had got the lifeboat ready and asked the keeper at the Rauer lighthouse to hail us when we approached and keep us there till a message could be sent in to him at Sandefjord. He would then set sail at once and meet us at Rauer.

This was the plan. But on the morning we passed Rauer the haze made it impossible for the lighthouse keeper to see us, and it must have seemed to the dentist's partner as if we had sailed past our biggest and best chance.

As things turned out, however, we had really been lucky, for the man who brought the fateful letter from Oslo was not a loyal Norwegian. He proved later to be one of the best informers the German Police at Sandefjord had in so-called Norwegian circles, and from the moment the dentist's letter arrived the owner of the *Bergen* was shadowed wherever he went.

When he heard from Rauer that in all probability the *Haabet* had sailed past, he set sail at once with the intention of taking the *Bergen* to England alone. But his movements were reported to the German Harbor Police, and next day he was arrested and the lifeboat confiscated.

After being released from several months' detention in the Grini Concentration Camp, this man made another attempt with the lifeboat *Stavanger,* which also was detected; but he managed to escape from German custody and at last succeeded in getting into Sweden and from there straight to England, where he joined the Norwegian forces.

There were crowds of Germans everywhere we went along the coast, both in large and small towns. But everywhere, too, there were people who were ready to give a helping hand when assistance was needed. People asked as a rule where we meant to go, and our reply was always, "West!" Of course "west" could mean anything, and we left it to people's intelligence to figure out for themselves what our plans were.

Our voyage had reached a harbor outside Kristiansand without any difficulties worth mentioning. In the last few days we had had pretty bad weather with a strong southwester, and this meant continual beating up against the wind. The *Haabet* was still as leaky as on the day we left Bestumkilen, but we had grown accustomed to it and bailed at regular intervals without paying any great attention to the troublesome task.

One question worried us, however: How would things go when we were compelled to sail both night and day? Would two men be able to stand the exertions alone if it blew a gale for any length of time?

This question could not be answered for the present.
We should have to wait and see.

Kristiansand was the Germans' great naval harbor,
and, in conjunction with Kjevik Airfield, the place held
great interest for us. One day when I was up on the
second floor of a building that afforded an excellent
view over the harbor and naval station, our great plans
for reaching England nearly came to a sudden end.

I had taken a number of photographs, and was just
about to thrust the camera under my shirt, when I
noticed a German sentry on the opposite pavement,
staring keenly up at me. It did not take me many
seconds to reach the first floor but the German was
just as quick. We collided in the corridor, and for a
few seconds I stood in confusion, searching for polite
German phrases with which to answer his barrage of
questions.

Had I been taking photographs? Did I not know
that it was strictly forbidden to take photographs of
German military positions and equipment? Had I not
heard the announcement that spies would be sentenced
to death immediately if caught in the act?

No, I had not the slightest idea of it. I came from
a farm far away in the countryside, was engaged in
timber-felling for the Germans, knew little of the regulations in force in a big town. All I wanted was a
souvenir of the splendid German Navy, the pearl of
the German services!

The conversation went on for a good quarter of an
hour, with the result that when we parted we were
the best of friends. I had invited the German to drink

a glass of beer with me at six the same evening and he told me that I might keep the film on condition that I promised to hide it till after the war (which, of course, the Germans were going to win) and not tell a soul that I had taken any photographs.

There is no need to say more than that I did not keep the appointment with the German sentry.

The same afternoon, as Kaare and I sat in the cabin eating our dinner, we heard over the radio the following announcement by the German High Command: "Any boat which from today onward attempts to escape from Norway, and crosses the boundaries laid down for coastal traffic by the German High Command, will be attacked by every means and sunk without warning!"

We were startled. Of course it was just what we had expected, but at the same time it was a blunt reminder which invited reflection. It was this warning—combined with my brush with the sentry earlier in the day—that made us decide to try to get away from Kristiansand the following night, abandon our proposed visits to Mandal and Farsund, and set our course direct for England.

But what about our papers and equipment as commercial travelers in case we were hailed or caught outside the permitted boundary? Something had to be done about this, and that "something" was a rapid change in our equipment and papers in the hours that followed. For this we owe our thanks to a tobacconist, "Abrahamsen on the Quay," a man with whom we had come into casual contact earlier. It did not take him long to obtain a complete fishing outfit, secondhand, and fishermen's passes which were filled in with proper identification marks of our eighteen-foot craft.

"Abrahamsen on the Quay" also obtained an American flag and a German flag which he thought might be useful. We ourselves had a British flag, sewn into the mattress.

At 1:00 A.M. the *Haabet* stood out from Kristiansand, with a light night breeze from the north. The sky was overcast and it was dark, but not too dark for us to see clearly the outlines of islets and rocks. We passed slowly between the various German fortifications. As we sat there working, not even daring to whisper to one another, our pace seemed even slower than it was.

We risked keeping to the middle of the waterway, because neither of us knew the submerged rocks in the channel and could not use too much light in consulting the chart. But all went well. We did not hear a sound from anywhere, and in two hours we had left behind us the last rocks of the skerries.

But fate decided to take a hand. The wind dropped, and dropped quickly. It was difficult to judge how far out we had got while it was dark. But we had an answer a few hours later. When it grew light the coast line appeared on the horizon; we had not come as far out as we had hoped. The sails hung flapping, and the boom swung in time with the boat's movements in the swell. Not a breath of wind! Kaare and I looked at each other and said nothing. It was a long way to England.

Then Kaare started up, stared, and pointed. "Look there!" I turned round, weary and worn after twenty-four hours without sleep. But what we both saw brought me to my senses more quickly than a bucket of ice-cold water could have! A German destroyer!

We heaved ourselves into our emergency equipment: out with the fishing lines!

There was no doubt about the destroyer's intention; she was making straight for us at full speed. Next moment two shots rang in quick succession, followed by two explosions in the water straight ahead of us.

The destroyer was slowing down, but Kaare and I continued to haul on our lines as if nothing had happened. A man shouted to us in German from the destroyer's bridge and ordered us to prepare for boarding. We continued to haul on the lines.

A boat was launched with three men in it; and soon we had the three on board—a lieutenant and two aides. There were no polite phrases this time! The lieutenant curtly ordered that the *Haabet* should be thoroughly searched, then he turned to Kaare and me. We both feared the worst. First, papers. Then, an explanation as to why we were so far out. We who had fishermen's passes ought to know that we were forbidden to go farther than one sea mile out.

It took us a long time to explain that we had started the evening before, that a dead calm and strong southward current had driven us far beyond where we had originally meant to fish, and that our engine had broken down. Curiously enough, the lieutenant believed our explanation, and when one of the two aides reported finding a whisky bottle, three-fourths full, there seemed to be no further doubt in the lieutenant's mind.

Till then we had been fearful that the Germans might discover the secret place in the tie beam which supported the cabin roof. But the whisky bottle seemed to have saved the situation! I took advantage of the interest momentarily aroused to ask the lieutenant if we could have a tow in toward the coast again, and he amiably agreed. He ordered his two subordinates back to the destroyer, which throughout the visit had had two machine guns trained on us.

The episode that followed was too comic ever to be forgotten. We went coastward in tow of the destroyer so fast that the water spurted up at our bows. On board the *Haabet* sat the lieutenant, Kaare, and I swallowing one drink after another. We made sure that the lieutenant's glass was full all the time.

The bottle was soon nearly empty, and Kaare and I pretended to be drunk. But the lieutenant actually was drunk as a lord! And the best part of the little party was an admirable rendition by three voices of the song the Germans, drunk with victory, were then singing: *"Denn wir fahren gegen Engeland!"* [We're on Our Way to England].

Off Mövika, three-and-a-half miles from Kristiansand, the destroyer stopped, a boat came over to pick up the intoxicated lieutenant, wishes for a good voyage were exchanged, and we set sail again, cruising westward with a freshening breeze. Evidently the destroyer had not acted on any information from German Naval Headquarters at Kristiansand; the whole incident was simply a routine apprehension of fishermen breaking the regulations.

We now took the risk of proceeding to Mandal, where our next task was to get pictures of Mandal Airfield and the surrounding area.

When we lay to at one of the wharves in the Mandal River, we caught sight of a dark, thickset fellow who stood leaning against a telegraph post, following us with his eyes. He seemed keenly interested in everything we did. We were now accustomed to expect almost anything, and Kaare called my attention to this fellow.

At regular intervals in the course of the next three days this man stood on the same spot and watched every one of our movements. When, on the third day, we began to set sail, he came up to the boat and introduced himself as Rolf Gabrielsen, bank clerk, living in Mandal. We chatted about one thing and another, till he suddenly asked if we wanted a third hand.

"A third hand? What for?" Kaare asked.

Well, he thought he could tell us exactly where we were headed for, after the preparations we had been making on board the boat and in view of our age and behavior! Without waiting for an answer, he went on to tell us that he had tried once before to get on a boat going to England, but that time the boat was overcrowded. Now it looked as if we could use a hand, and it was his greatest wish to get over to the other side and report for duty.

Without our asking for any, he gave us a number of

references in Mandal; among them was a leader of
one of the former Mandal Scout troops, whom I had
met a few years before.

Of course neither Kaare nor I gave him an inkling
of our real intentions. We insisted we had no plans
for a voyage to England. We were professional fishermen and meant to go on to Bergen. Gabrielsen accepted our statement, but remarked before leaving
us that he was ready to do anything he could to help
us, then he departed.

A long and thorough discussion took place that afternoon in the *Haabet's* cabin. We wanted a third hand;
there was no chance of our holding out for several
days on end if we ran into a gale on the way over.
Certainly there was not room for three in the cabin
at one time, but the problem would not arise once
the voyage really started.

Among the many people Gabrielsen had given us
as references were two who we knew were good Norwegians—and safe. The same evening I went up to
see one of them and cleared up the question of Gabrielsen's identity. He was a first-class man who knew
something about sailing.

That was enough for us. Rolf Gabrielsen moved on
board the *Haabet* next day as the third member of
the crew. At five in the afternoon all was ready, the
necessary photographs had been taken so far as time
allowed, a final overhaul of the *Haabet* had been
made, the forehatch covered with canvas and securely
battened down, and a thick tarpaulin drawn on solid
trestles over the greater part of the open cockpit,
leaving only a small hole open for the steersman.

We hoped that in case of severe weather any water which might wash over the deck would be prevented from getting into the boat. That was the theory! A fresh supply of water was taken on board, and for safety's sake we asked Gabrielsen to get fifteen bottles of seltzer as an extra supply.

It was still blowing hard from the southwest when we set our course that evening for Lindesnes, the most southerly point of Norway on the mainland. It was the same wind which had hindered our progress all the way down the coast. Southwest was just the direction in which we should sail to get across to England, and the wind was dead against us. We agreed, therefore, to drop anchor for the night in a sheltered little creek between Mandal and Lindesnes, which Rolf knew from earlier times, and proceed the next day.

We dropped anchor at 11:00 P.M. in a little Southern Norway paradise well hidden amid a ring of wooded islets. All was still; only occasional gusts from a gentle night breeze reached us. It was mild and rather muggy, and for more than an hour we lay on deck talking over prospects.

We sailed again early next morning. The same wretched weather continued: southwest wind and rough sea. The wind kept rising during the day, and when we rounded Lindesnes it was blowing hard, and we had to shorten sail. Earlier that morning we had considered sailing straight from Lindesnes with England as our next stop, but weather conditions put an end to that. As the wind grew stronger the sea rose, the *Haabet* was tossed up and down like a nutshell, and all three of us had our first taste of seasickness.

There were no protests, therefore, when I announced that we were going to put into Farsund as quickly as possible.

The next day was Friday, September 13, so of course we did not even consider departing that day. Besides, we had plenty to do investigating the proposed new airfield at Lista; and through some of Rolf's connections we obtained considerable material about it.

Saturday, September 14, 1940, broke with just the weather we wanted. Easterly wind, overcast, fresh breeze. It could not have been better if we had ordered it. Before long all was ready, and then came the cry, "Cast off!"

I shall never forget the sail that followed. We went like smoke down the fjord from Farsund, and soon we decided to run close-reefed. The wind had increased to a strong breeze and we shot out in a wild dash toward the open sea. This was what we had been waiting for—a wind which would blow us in the right direction either under or above the surface!

One of the Lifeboat Society's well-known smacks emerged from among some islands to starboard, also close-reefed. The water foamed about the proud vessel's bow as she swung up toward us. If only we had a craft like that! We all had the same thought as we stood in the steering cockpit dripping wet from the spray which swept in over us. The lifeboat came up alongside, set the same course as ours, and started a race the like of which none of us had taken part in before.

The *Haabet* was in her element. In this kind of sailing there were not many boats that could beat her. A man on board the lifeboat hung in the rigging with a megaphone to his lips. "All under control?" he called.

"Couldn't be better!" I shouted back at the top of my voice to make myself heard over the noise of the rushing sea and howling wind.

Then the man yelled back through his megaphone: "Good luck and wish them all the best on the other side!"

We stood for a few moments too surprised to say a word. It was strange how well-informed the fellow seemed to be, and it was disquieting, too. But a moment later our suspicions vanished; the lifeboat was dipping the Norwegian flag to us. Kaare crept forward along the deck to the mast and dipped our Norwegian flag in return.

This was a great and stirring moment, for the fateful voyage had begun! The lifeboat altered course inshore again, and soon we were alone on the rough sea, a nutshell abandoned to the will and whims of the forces of nature.

"All under control?" That was a question we were to ask ourselves many times that day. With a thirty-knot wind on her beam, the *Haabet* showed herself at her best. The water poured incessantly over the deck, and the man at the helm had a hard job keeping the boat on an even keel. We sailed and pumped, pumped and sailed; gradually and surely the coast line astern of us grew fainter and fainter.

Kaare was at the helm, Rolf pumping, and I sitting in the cabin trying to light the primus stove. We were

all hungry and it was time to eat, but this was easier
said than done. Inside the cabin there was chaos, ship's
stores and personal belongings being flung about between the bulkheads. The *Haabet* pitched and rolled
in the heavy seas, and I had to sit down to keep a
tight hold on both primus and cooking pot.

"You'd better come out if you want to say good-by
to old Mother Norway; the coast line's just disappearing below the horizon!" Kaare shouted through the
cabin door. Rolf and I dropped what we were doing
and crawled out to the steersman's post. The jagged
mountains of Norway were just vanishing below the
horizon. Not a word was spoken. Each of us had his
own thoughts. Were we looking at those mountains
for the last time? How long would it be before we
again saw that land which we loved so much?

Suddenly Kaare yelled, "Look!" We followed the
direction of his outstretched hand. A plane—two
planes! We all three stood staring for a few seconds.
They were coming out toward us—they had seen us!
"Out with the lines! Back the sail!"

Before I could get the order carried out, Kaare
dashed into the cabin and came out again a moment
later dragging the smallest of our two fishing lines.
Over the side went the line, and a minute later, when
the planes reached us, we were busy hauling on it.
They were two German Heinkel 115's. For a few
breathless minutes they circled around the *Haabet*,
which was now flying the German swastika flag together with the Norwegian.

We continued to work at our lines, but found time

to wave to the airmen with a white cloth, while the *Haabet* heaved up and down in the rough sea with backed sails. The planes grazed the masthead three times, then circled and finally dropped two red flares outside us. To emphasize their meaning, one of the planes came in on a last run and fired a salvo of machine-gun bullets hardly ten yards from us—between us and England. Then they zoomed away again while we stood literally gasping for breath.

Was that all, or was it only the beginning? It seemed, however, that they were satisfied, for they both disappeared landward and were lost in a heavy shower of rain which was approaching from the eastward. "In with the lines!" And our mad career continued.

Now the big question was whether the planes would report our position; if they did, we could expect a visit from a German coast patrol. If that happened the result was clear. We were far outside the permitted zone. But fate was kind to us. Soon afterward an unbroken cover of mist and rain moved in toward the coast, and we could not see for more than a few hundred yards in any direction. Only rough sea and low rain-filled storm clouds.

Darkness came on slowly, and with it the wind increased. I shall never forget that first night on board an eighteen-foot sailing boat in the North Sea. Sleep for any of us was out of the question; it took all our efforts just to keep the little craft afloat. The wind increased steadily and surely, and it looked to us as if the *Haabet* was more underwater than above it.

Every other hour the cabin floor was submerged,

and it was not long before practically everything inside the little cabin was soaking wet. With every movement caused by the heavy sea, the water on board was flung up above the bulkheads, spurted over everything that was not covered up, and ran down into the bottom again. While I took the wheel during the first half of the night, Kaare managed to cook a fairly decent meal over the primus. Rolf had a full-time job pumping, and, when this was not necessary, replacing all the things which had been flung about the cabin by the boat's violent motion.

At 11:20 that night the mainsail split across, along one of the seams by the third reef. The noise was like a pistol shot, and for a good half-hour Kaare and I lay out on the cabin roof, lashed fast, trying to fix things up as best we could. But finally we had to give up. The wind was too strong, and running before it under the foresail alone was enough that night.

Gradually but surely, one defect after another was discovered, things which ought to have been put right before we started. Now it was too late; all we could do was make the best of the situation. Our fighting spirit, which had asserted itself earlier in the day, had disappeared.

All of us had the same thought: If only I had known better than to come on this voyage in such a boat! Instead, we all tried to make light of the serious situation, tried to convince one another that these matters were all trifles. But not one of us was deceived; we all three realized that things were dead-serious.

Never before have the hours and minutes of a night

been so long. Everything was dark. We could only hear the rushing of the wind and the roaring of the seas that broke incessantly over the little craft. But in spite of everything we sent up fervent thanks to Him who had arranged this weather. What should we have done if the same wind had come from the west?

4 We Battle the North Sea

WHEN AT LAST the day of September 15 dawned, we were all three dead-tired after the physical and mental strain of navigating a boat like the *Haabet* in the darkness. What a night! And this was only the first!

During the three days and nights that followed there was no need to repair the mainsail. We ran westward with our foresail filled. Our speed was more than satisfactory and the direction of the wind perfect. Slowly and surely we became accustomed to life on board ship; slowly and surely we learned what it was like to sail the sea in a small leaky boat. What we at first thought was a gale was little more than a fresh breeze, but we learned it was enough for both the *Haabet* and ourselves.

Now and then, during the daylight hours, each man in turn managed to get a half-hour's nap on one of the bunks in the cabin; real, honest-to-goodness sleep was out of the question, the boat's sudden movements were too violent for that. But we kept afloat, and mile after mile vanished in our wake.

Our direction? We had at last set up a kind of compass in gimbals on the engine casing, an old compass

Kaare had got hold of before we left Oslo. Curiously enough, this compass served us well on the voyage across, though we paid little attention to deviation or other metallic influence on the magnetic needle. The direction was west-southwest, and we kept pretty well to it.

On the third day, however, something happened which shook us out of any complacency. A heavy sea suddenly flung the boat over on one side. The motion was so violent that it flung the watertight bottle containing matches and tinder, which had its regular place upon one of the shelves, against a bulkhead on the lee side, smashing it into a thousand pieces.

The contents were thrown about the cabin and most of them ended up in the water, which was already over the floor. Strong language didn't help much. For more than two hours Kaare and Rolf were busy drying matches in the frying pan over the primus, an activity that was to occupy a lot of their time later on.

We had been at sea for four days and nights when, on the morning of September 18, the weather began to change. The wind dropped steadily, and at twelve o'clock it was gentle enough so we could make ourselves heard without shouting. What next? Actually, we had so much repair work to do that we did not waste time worrying about the future.

All the clothes on board, and every stitch we wore, had been wet through for the last two days, and this opportunity of drying our clothes was a welcome interlude. Moreover, the weather at last gave us a chance to rest a little. We were all dead-tired after our exertions and anxiety, and while one man was on watch, the other two were able to get a few hours' sleep.

Stockings, underclothes, outerclothes, and sleeping bags were hung up wherever there was room, and for the next few hours the *Haabet* looked like an untidy fishing smack. I myself set about repairing the mainsail, and before long we were under full sail again.

But that did not help us much. The sails hung and swung round the rigging, and at last we were forced to lash the mainsail boom because it threatened to knock us overboard. The swell was still running high, and strangely, now for the first time since Farsund, the earliest symptoms of seasickness appeared. First Rolf was laid low, then I, and lastly Kaare.

The only thing that had kept us from being sick before was probably the tension under which we had been; none of us had had time to be sick. But we made up for it now. We all felt wretched the whole day.

It was Kaare who at half-past four that afternoon roused me from a nightmare I was having while trying to get a nap in the cabin. I was dreaming of waves higher than a house and a little nutshell of a boat when the cry, "Plane!" rang in my ears. I heaved myself out of my sleeping bag, crawled out on deck, and there— in the direction indicated by Kaare's outstretched arm —was a little black dot against a deep-blue sky.

"Get the British flag that's sewn up in the mattress!" I yelled the order, and Kaare disappeared into the cabin like a streak of lightning and returned a moment later with the Union Jack in his hand. We yelled, hooted, waved with everything we had. The dot against the sky in the west grew larger and larger. Yes, it looked as if the plane had seen us, but what kind of a plane was it—friend or enemy?

We stared at the dot till our eyes almost popped out of our heads. Why, what was he doing? Hadn't he seen us? We stopped our wild gesturing and stood gaping open-mouthed. The plane swung westward, grew smaller and smaller—and disappeared.

I'm not ashamed to confess that I was close to tears as I looked at the faces of Kaare and Rolf. Not that my own was any better. For a few unforgettable moments toil and fear were totally forgotten in a hope which seemed on the verge of fulfillment. It must have been a British plane so far out. We could not be far from the Scottish or English coast after the last four days' sailing.

It was no good crying; it was a good sign and we could only hope for better luck next time. But what made us angry with ourselves was that not till it was over did we remember the three rockets we had stolen from a German dump before we left Oslo for use in just such a case.

Rolf was now put on watch while Kaare and I tried to sleep. What lay before us no one knew; the worst could still happen.

We were awakened by Rolf shouting: "Ship!"

Again we rushed out, and there, above the horizon in the west, rose a little cloud of smoke. There wasn't any doubt, it must be a ship! Again we worked ourselves up into a triumphant mood; again we were doomed to disappointment. For a good hour the column of smoke continued to rise above the horizon from the "something" which we all hoped so desperately would materialize into a ship. At last there was no longer any smoke, and with the smoke vanished our hope.

It was now past six, and the sails still hung flapping around the rigging. Not a breath of wind! The sun had gone down in the west, and we had taken the opportunity to check the compass. All three of us were sitting on deck; we had almost forgotten what had happened in the last few hours, and were watching the brilliant spectacle in the western sky, where the sun had sunk into the sea, leaving behind it a river of red.

I myself was thinking of what awaited us behind that horizon, what the future might bring to us all, what the future might bring to the world.

Then it was my turn to start. A sound—a distant buzz. "Plane!" I yelled. And there, in the midst of the blood-red river the sunset had left, was a tiny dot which steadily increased in size! We were all a little more reasonable this time, took it more quietly, because by now we were all pretty skeptical as to the result.

The Union Jack was spread over the cabin roof, which was white and provided a good background for the bright colors in the flag. Two of the three flares were got ready; if they did not succeed this time it was a good thing to have one in reserve for later. We sent up one flare.

Again we stood and stared. Yes, the dot in the west grew gradually and surely; we began to distinguish details. It was a double-engined plane. Nearer—nearer —it *must* see us, it *must!*

I let off another rocket; it shot upward into the air, burst high up, and three red lights drifted slowly down toward us. We stared and stared at the plane. Yes—it *had* seen us! We cheered, danced about the deck, waved back with every strip of cloth and flag we had.

The plane, a twin-engined Avro Anson, came roaring over the *Haabet*. What a sight! Twice it swept past us on a level with the masthead, so near that we could make out the crew on board, could see them waving. Then they began to fly in a narrow circle around us and to send a message by signal lamp.

None of us were at first capable of receiving any message, nor did the message matter so long as they had seen us! But they repeated their signals, and at last we got a receiving station organized—Kaare took down the message while I dictated dots and dashes. At the speed at which they sent I could make out only a few of the letters; the rest we would have to find out afterward. I clung tight to the rigging with a signal flag in each hand.

"Will report your position and arrange for rescue!"

I sent back three times: "Have escaped from Norway using call sign *D* for David thank you!"

For more than twenty minutes the plane continued to fly round us in now wider, now narrower circles, and as a last farewell it came roaring down over the *Haabet* at full speed. Our jubilation can be imagined! All weariness was gone, the toil and struggle with the elements forgotten; there was only one thing that counted—we were going to be picked up by a British ship, perhaps that same evening, or certainly early next morning!

It was almost incredible! The inward doubt which had pursued us since the day we sailed from Oslo, the doubt which had grown stronger with each day and night that passed, was now suddenly gone. This was reality; we had been seen by a British plane and it had reported us!

Our seasickness was gone, too, and before the plane had disappeared on the horizon we had decided unanimously that the occasion called for a celebration. We had not much in the way of extras, but in a little while we were all three sitting on deck, eating bread soaked in salt water, thickly spread with butter and sardines!

At seven-thirty that evening we suddenly noticed wind in the sails. As we lay at ease on deck with our pipes in our mouths, chattering about the great possibilities which had now so suddenly become almost reality, we saw thick, dark cloud banks in the west. The *Haabet* heaved regularly and steadily in the swell, which now seemed to be coming in from all sides.

We sat and stared. The faint breeze which now began to fill the sails came from the westward! The black cloud banks were approaching us slowly but surely. We looked at each other—and said nothing. All three of us felt the menace those clouds held.

The wind increased. We began to beat up against it. The best course the *Haabet* managed to keep was southwest by south. We agreed to sail for exactly half an hour on each tack, courses southwest by south and northwest by west.

The wind increased; the seas began to drive in from the west, growing gradually higher as the hours passed. But there was still only a light breeze and we tried to assure one another that it was nothing to worry about; we had a sea anchor (a present from our friend the dentist), and this change of wind would certainly not continue for long.

At 9:00 P.M. the wind had increased to a fresh breeze, and it was fairly dark now. We had to choose between taking in sail in case the weather grew rough during the night or lying to with a sea anchor. We chose the latter. It was pretty certain that the plane had reported us, and even if we drifted a short distance in the course of the night, a vessel of any size would be quite sure to find us.

The sea anchor was sort of large funnel, made of solid canvas with a small hole in the end of it, and mounted on a frame of thin steel. An old corked kerosene can served as a buoy to hold this up at a fixed depth below the surface. The whole sea anchor was attached to a 100-foot chain, and as it had originally been made for a lifeboat there was no doubt that it would hold us in more or less the same place through the night.

Rolf took the first watch, while Kaare and I turned in to try to get a little sleep. We had by now grown accustomed to the steady heaving and soon we both were sleeping.

At 11:30 P.M. we were awakened by a shout from

Rolf: "The wind's getting higher! The sea's beginning to go white!" We had hardly gotten out of our sleeping bags when the next warning shout came: "The anchor chain's broken!" At the same moment we were both flung against one of the bulkheads: things were getting serious!

Without a word we crept through the cabin opening. It was pitch-dark and we couldn't see a thing. We felt our way forward to where Rolf stood hauling in a loose, broken chain. We had to act quickly. We must set sail, close-reefed, and try to beat up against the wind, or try to lie to, head to wind.

Only someone who has tried to set sail on a boat with no steerageway on her on a pitch-dark night in the North Sea will fully understand the labor and difficulties this involves. For a half-hour we struggled desperately with sails and halyards, reefs and rope-ends, before we were able to get the sails set satisfactorily.

The attempt to get the boat to lie head to wind soon proved hopeless. We had no sooner got her steady than a heavy sea poured over us and drove us off our course, with the result that we got the wind right on our beam and came near being forced under. There was nothing else to do but try to beat up against the wind.

What sailing! The *Haabet*, with close-reefed sails, lay almost flat with half the deck continually under water. It was impossible to see forward to the bow, much less ahead of it, so as to avoid the worst breaking seas. Two of us hung onto the tiller and tried to keep the boat's head to the wind.

Spray flew over us, and the noise of the seething, boiling seas, coupled with the howling of the wind, grew steadily wilder. Sea after sea poured over the tiny nutshell, each time threatening to capsize us; we were shaken, tossed violently up and down, to and fro, like a leaf in a storm.

"We'll go to the bottom if it continues like this!" I yelled across to Kaare. "We'll have to take in the mainsail!"

Before I had finished the sentence, nature gave the answer. With a noise like the crack of a gun, we heard the mainsail go; in seconds it was split right across, a reef higher than the time before!

"Take the tiller!" I shouted to Rolf.

With Kaare, I slithered along to the mast and clung tightly to it at the very moment when a fresh sea poured over us. I took a gulp of sea water and for a moment lay gasping for breath. Yes, Kaare was still on board, desperately clutching the cabin roof. The mainsail was thrashing in the wind and it was no easy task to recover the strips. But we managed it; we got the remains lashed fast to the mainsail boom and finally lashed up the boom properly. Meanwhile Rolf did a miraculous job of keeping the *Haabet* hove to under her backed foresail.

For a good half-hour we kept going, beating up against the wind under the close-reefed foresail. But the *Haabet* would not sail in this manner under prevailing conditions, as she had shown herself capable of doing in a gentle breeze outside the skerries. It was impossible to get up any speed, for as soon as she began to slide down into the trough of the waves and to get a little way on her, the next wave top came pouring over her and put a stop to each attempt. It was hopeless.

To make matters worse, the *Haabet* now was leaking twice as fast as before. Rolf investigated the new leak with a flashlight and soon reported that the water was spurting in through new cracks along the tabernacle in the bottom of the boat.

While Rolf was caulking the leaks, a fresh sea came rushing over us. Kaare and I, hanging onto the tiller, could hear its approaching roar. Before we were sure of its direction it was upon us, and for a few seconds everything was submerged in a seething mass of water.

We were in imminent danger of capsizing. But that wasn't all; when the boat rose again and we had spat out enough sea water to be able to call to one another, Kaare and I discovered that we were clinging to a smashed tiller. There was nothing to be done about it. Another sea like that, and we were done for.

"Get up the spare tiller on the starboard side!" I yelled to Rolf under the tarpaulin. Meanwhile Kaare hung over the stern of the boat and vainly tried to steer with the little stump that was left. And now, about turn! We had no choice but to run before the wind. I shouted the order, fully aware of what it meant: back the same way we had come!

As the night gradually wore on, the weather grew steadily worse and the wind reached what in meteorological language is called "a moderate gale." We had rigged up a little storm sail from the foresail, set crossways on the forecastle, and astern we had hung out a "warp" about sixty feet long made of the remains of the anchor chain and some thick rope we had brought along for emergency use. We figured this would provide a fairly good brake on the fantastic speed we were sure to reach with the wind coming from behind us.

When dawn came at last, the *Haabet* and her crew presented a sorry spectacle: a nutshell completely abandoned to the forces of nature, rigged with the ludicrous little storm sail forward; the crew, three shadows of themselves. Back we went in a wild chase with wind and sea astern of us—the same course we had covered in four-and-a-half days—fighting desperately to stay afloat.

Gone was all hope of being saved, at any rate in the next day or two. If this weather continued much longer, we could not possibly keep from going under. That fact was more and more strongly emphasized as the hours passed. The *Haabet* leaked like a sieve; every hour fresh cracks along the tabernacle were discovered, cracks through which the water spurted in faster than any pump could clear it out again.

Rolf caulked desperately. Kaare and I worked shifts at the tiller. As skipper I felt my responsibilty strongly; I alone was responsible for the complete disaster which now seemed inevitable.

For four days and nights the storm continued without interruption; for four days we fought for our lives, fought to avoid the worst seas, fought to keep the water inboard below the level of the cabin floor. But every time a sea struck us at a wrong angle, the water poured in through the opening in the tarpaulin where the steersman stood, and whoever was at the pump floundered in sea water for the next few minutes while working at high pressure.

Now, from sheer exhaustion, we had reached the stage where one becomes dull-witted, indifferent to what is happening except when the situation becomes crucial. Everything was soaked—clothes, mattresses, and sleeping bags; we had not a scrap of dry clothing to change into. We froze day and night till our teeth chattered, but we no longer noticed it. None of us had had a minute's sleep in four days; our hands were swollen with sea water, and struggling with halyards and sheets had removed what little skin we had left.

Rolf, who had come straight from a bank stool, without even the little preliminary training Kaare and I had had, went about with hands which looked like lumps of raw meat.

Toward morning on Setember 23, death came knocking at the door in earnest. This was the night none of us would ever forget, even though we never really knew how we managed to remain alive.

It was past midnight and pitch-dark. In the last three hours the wind seemed to have increased in fury. Kaare and I were at the tiller, while Rolf lay under the tarpaulin, pumping. The water was now over the cabin floor every twenty minutes, and whatever caulking we did was almost futile. It was the steady pressure on the rigging that kept pushing down the foot of the mast; soon it would probably go right through the bottom.

It was not only the giant waves now which broke

over the boat at regular intervals; the wind whirled the sea up, and from every wave top, great or small, the water poured over us like a waterfall. It lashed our faces and filled our eyes all the time we were trying to look astern and steer to avoid the worst seas.

We could see absolutely nothing, but in the last few days we had learned to rely on sound and nothing else. The rushing noise from the seas, growing louder and louder as they approached, finally rising to a bellowing roar, was the only thing by which we could judge where the waves came from. If it was too late to steer out of their way, what happened next depended on how quickly the steersman could judge the direction, in order to take the sea on board exactly in the direction in which it was moving.

This applied also to the frightful seconds that followed, during which the boat was heaved up with the wave at a fearful pace, completely buried in it. If the boat sheered away, the water poured in and the *Haabet* heeled over on one side. Then the great question was whether it would ever come up again.

We hung onto the tiller and fought desperately to keep the vessel on an even keel. Seas tumbled in over us, each bigger than the last. Rolf had just finished pumping, and I shouted in to him to come out and take Kaare's place. Meanwhile Kaare crept into the cabin to fill three oil bags with oil to throw onto the sea; our last remaining hope was that the oil would prevent the seas from breaking over us. I could barely hear myself giving the orders, it was all I could do to utter the words.

Rolf and I were lashed fast to the rail to keep from being knocked overboard. The now familiar roaring came from the darkness behind us. We both automatically yelled a warning to the man in the cabin: "Hold tight! Sea!"

Neither Rolf nor I had any idea where the sea was coming from before it tumbled on board. Everything was carried away. The tiller was torn out of my hands, there was a fearful roaring which seemed to deaden all other sounds: water—sea—we're sinking—sinking—sinking!

I tried in vain to breathe, only gulped down bitter salt sea water—everything was black—and curiously quiet. I felt myself rising slowly, my lungs nearly bursting—then I felt the wind tearing at my hair again and I gasped for air. My life belt had done its job! At the same time I felt the rope from the *Haabet* tight around my waist, and slowly I dragged myself on board. But the *Haabet* lay broadside onto the sea, half-full of water, and now it was only a question of seconds.

Just as I climbed on board, Rolf came up on the other side. We had been washed overboard when the big sea passed over us. But what had happened to Kaare? I yelled in but got no answer. I shouted to Rolf to break up the deck planks he was standing on in the steering hole. Then I crawled into the cabin, tumbled over Kaare as he tried to drag himself up onto one of the bunks half-conscious, got hold of the bag I was searching for, and paddled out again.

There was no time to help Kaare, or to find out what had happened; we must bail—bail—bail!

But where was the tiller? Rolf yelled across to me that it had been carried away by the big sea. In a few seconds two of the deck planks were fastened together around the upper part of the rudder; this would have to hold until we had an opportunity of repairing it properly—if we got another chance. But something else was lacking too. We had completely lost steerage control and speed; we just lay tumbling up and down broadside onto the seas.

Then Kaare came scrambling out of the cabin. He managed to explain in a feeble voice that he had been flung against the bulkhead and knocked unconscious. He had come to after swallowing a few quarts of sea water.

"The storm sail must have gone!" I yelled across to Kaare. Before I could say anything more, he disappeared in the direction of the bow, clinging to the cabin roof. It was madness; if a big wave came now Kaare would not have a chance. But there was no time to waste. We went on bailing feverishly. Then we noticed that the *Haabet* was under sail again; and Kaare came crawling back.

"The foresail wire's gone. I've hoisted the storm sail on the peak halyard. All under control!"

This was just like Kaare. When everything looked blackest, he could always find something to joke about.

All under control! But it was not to be for many minutes. Kaare disappeared into the cabin again to continue where he had left off. A few seconds after he had vanished, a fresh sea came tumbling on board. This time neither Rolf nor I received full warning.

Once more everything seemed to have gone, but we both managed to stay aboard by hanging on fiercely to what we now called the tiller.

The *Haabet* sheered away and heeled over on her side, and when at last we were able to breathe again, we were both hanging halfway over the rail up to our waists in the water. But what was even worse, the boat was lying with her mast in the water and the sea pouring in though the open steering hole.

What I yelled to Rolf I do not remember; I only know that next moment we were hanging on the weather side as tightly as we could, and a moment later Kaare was beside us. Slowly the *Haabet* rose again, this time three-quarters full of water.

Once more we bailed—bailed as we had never bailed before. Kaare tried to use the pump, but this was full of scraps of paper from a stack of *Fritt Folk*. These Nazi newspapers had been lying on a shelf and had now dissolved in the sea water. I used the bucket on one side and Rolf his own sou'wester on the other, but the situation was hopeless.

We had not got the water inboard down even to floor level when the third giant wave came tumbling over us. All I know it that I let out a yell as something struck me a hard blow on the forehead. Then everything became curiously still. I held my breath automatically, felt the boat being forced down and myself somehow getting underneath her and sinking ever deeper and deeper. My ears filled with a deep rushing noise. Then I was coming up to the surface again.

I can remember that I was clinging to the weather

side with Kaare, that the *Haabet* rose again and Rolf was dragged on board, and that we bailed. But what happened in detail, and how, I do not know. One thing I remember clearly: I called to Kaare and asked him to pray with me! And at the moment when we went down for the third time I clearly recollect seeing my mother's face before me; she was talking quietly and calmly, as she always did. And through the deafening roar of the storm and the sea I could hear her words distinctly:

"With God's help it'll go all right!"

Kaare and I stopped bailing; we knelt on the broken deck and prayed, while the seas continued to rush over us.

What happened after that I shall never forget. The third sea was the last which struck us in the wrong position. We seemed all the time to be lying in dead water. Wave after wave rushed past us, now to starboard, now to port. Many smaller seas broke on board, but they were all of a less dangerous kind.

The gale continued for four days longer. Eight days of full gale! Kaare was in very bad shape for more than a day after the worst night. When the *Haabet* heeled over he had struck his head against the bulkhead several times, and he had swallowed quarts of salt water as he lay unconscious on the floor of the flooded cabin. Rolf had not a scrap of skin left on his hands; they were swollen and full of deep cracks. I was not much better off myself.

Kaare remained lying in the cabin for the rest of the night, but by morning he managed to get on his legs again. I was at the helm for thirteen hours straight that night and the following day. Time after time, as the minutes and hours crept away, I almost collapsed at the bottom of the steering hole. But each time a new sea came along to keep me awake.

When dawn came the *Haabet* was a pitiful sight, more so inside than out. The oil which Kaare had tried to pour into the bags had run over and been flung all over the bulkheads and ceiling along with the water that was on board. Everything was covered with a thin layer of grease, and the three of us had to develop the art of balance all over again in the days that followed. But this was not all.

The big water container, a glass bottle in a straw basket, which had been lashed firmly to one of the bulkheads, had broken loose, probably when the boat was on her beam ends for the second time, and inside the smashed bottle lay the scanty remains of what should have been our iron ration of fresh water. Now all we had left was a quart and a half of fresh water in a wooden keg which fortunately had withstood the upheaval. The fifteen bottles of seltzer which Rolf had brought on board at Mandal, and which also were to serve in an emergency, were smashed.

All the bread we possessed was completely ruined by salt water, and our food supply now consisted of four tins of sardines and a keg containing a little more than two pounds of that good mountain butter of my mother's! The situation seemed pretty hopeless.

On the following night, when Kaare was at the helm, there was a sudden shout of "Light ahead!" For only a moment hope flickered within us, but after we had

watched the light for a short time, that hope faded—
the light came from a lighthouse. It flashed steadily—
one long and two short! It could only be the Danish
coast.

Two hours later we saw another light, and while this
was visible we had a serious discussion in the steering
hole aft. Should we continue straight toward the light,
and give up now while safety was in sight? With our
storm sail full it would probably not take many hours
to reach it. But what would happen if we landed in
Denmark, occupied by the Germans? Undoubtedly we
should all three be captured by the Nazis and sent
back to Norway for trial. The result of that trial could
hardly be in doubt.

Was all we had gone through in the last five days, indeed in the nine-and-a-half days since we had left
Norway, to end so disastrously? Was the whole of our
plan to collapse?

On the other hand, how long could we continue this
nightmare, without water, food, or sleep?

Summing up, we found that the choice lay between
two kinds of death—being put up against a wall and
shot, or finding a common grave in the depths of the
North Sea. Further, there was still just a vestige of
hope that we might meet a British vessel somewhere
out here, especially if we managed to keep a more
westerly course.

We discussed the matter, weighing every single
point for and against, and came to a unanimous decision: either down to our graves in the North Sea, or
England.

It was not hard for a "skipper" to keep his courage

up when he had such a crew! Despite toil, thirst, cold, and everything else, there was complete agreement.

We continued our wild chase before the wind and sea.

The wind had now shifted more to the north, and it was easier for us to keep a more southwesterly course. We took in the long driving line and the brake we had hanging out astern. Had it not been for this piece of gear, based on good advice from our friend the dentist, we would have been less fortunate than we were.

We had no reason to complain of our speed; the water foamed about us, and at night the phosphorescence stood like a shining curtain over our bow. The sea was less rough now; the big waves gradually became smaller and fewer, but there was still no question of trying to run due west.

Late on the night of September 24, we had another bad fright. Rolf was at the helm while Kaare and I were sitting in the cabin for a moment, trying vainly to find a dry match. Everything in the way of tobacco was long ago soaked through, but we hoped to dry a little of it on the primus. Then Rolf shouted: "Mines!"

We dropped what we had in our hands and tumbled out. There! Hardly four yards from us a big horned mine sailed by! Rolf was hanging onto the improvised tiller and had already succeeded in twisting the *Haabet* out of the way. But was this the only one?

Low tattered storm clouds swept by over our heads; now and then, where the layer of clouds was thin, a full moon shone through. This doubtless was the last part of the gale passing over. While Kaare took over Rolf's job at the helm, Rolf crawled forward along the deck and remained sitting half-erect in the bow, holding tight to the forestay. Again he shouted: "Mines!"

Kaare heaved at the tiller and again we just missed a horned mine—number two. It was the fifth mine we had seen in all the voyage, but none of the earlier ones had been so uncomfortably near.

In the state we all three were now in, the effect on our morale was worse than it would normally have been. We strained our eyes out into the darkness, and everywhere we saw mines. Again and again Rolf yelled: "Mines!" But no more mines were seen.

Rolf was on the verge of collapse. "I see mines everywhere," he half-sobbed. "I can't stand this much longer."

It was not surprising that Rolf was the first to go nearly mad. The last time we were flung overboard, he was almost unconscious when we got him onto the boat again. Besides this, he had suffered a violent blow on the back of his head. Also, he was a less experienced seaman than Kaare and I; consequently, he worked a good deal harder.

From then on Rolf did nothing but pump. Every twenty minutes in the last three days, and every quarter of an hour on the last day of the voyage, Rolf pumped the *Haabet* clear. It was a wearisome task, and I shall never forget how faithfully he discharged it.

Whenever he had finished a turn, he sank down on the cabin floor between the two bunks, dozed off for twenty minutes, and woke up again when the water stood well above the cabin floor. By then the water was washing over his face and covered the greater part of his body. Several times we had to shout to him for fear he would drown where he lay. But Rolf pumped.

On September 28, early in the morning, the wind for the first time in eight days had dropped enough so we could repair the sails on board. While Kaare stood at the helm and we ran due southwest under a fore-staysail, I set about sewing together the two parts of the mainsail. It was not as simple as it sounds, soaking wet as the canvas was, and with hands and fingers swollen and sore.

There was another thing that worried us a great deal. The wire we had put in as a foresail halyard before leaving Norway had been carried away, and the remains had been torn out of the block up at the masthead. How should we put in a new foresail halyard?

Once more it was Kaare who saved the situation. A little later in the day he was hoisted up to the masthead with the help of the peak halyard and put in a new foresail halyard. It was a remarkable performance on his part—to be able, in the state he was in, to get to the masthead of a small sailing boat in the middle of the North Sea, heaved now to one side, now to the other, by the swell.

But it was done—a last gigantic effort on Kaare's part. And it cost him all the strength he had left. He lay in the cabin for the rest of the day, hardly able to move.

The *Haabet* was under sail again; westward, always

westward. But we had little strength left, and this was
our last chance. If the wind remained where it was,
we might make it. I sat aft in the steering hole, dozing
off now and again. Sometimes I was awakened when
the boat got too far into the wind so that her sails
flapped. It was still hard sailing, but nothing like what
we had in the previous eight days. We had had
nothing to eat of late but butter and sardines; two
sardines each at every meal. And our fresh water had
run out long ago.

The evening of the thirteenth day drew in. Kaare
relieved me at the helm, and Rolf was pumping. The
night was cold, with a bright starry sky; at about one
the moon rose. I was sitting out in the steering hole
with Kaare, and the hours passed without a word.
Now and then I dozed off, only to wake each time a
bigger wave struck the boat's side to lift us high.
Every fourth hour we changed places, and the man
who had the tiller tried to concentrate on compass
needles and course. Westward, always westward.

Rolf kept pumping.

September 29 dawned with sunshine and warmer
weather. As the day advanced, the wind increased a
little and became more easterly. We were sailing free
again under close-reefed sails. We had butter for
lunch; the sardines were gone. Hardly a word was
spoken. We were all thirsty, and the hope that the
day would bring a little rain soon disappeared. The
sun shone from a cloudless sky.

Westward, always westward.

I was sitting at the tiller. Kaare was stretched out

near me, asleep; Rolf was lying inside the cabin and
the water was already halfway up his pillow. It was
2:35 P.M. I was just going to give Rolf the usual warning shout, "You must pump!" when something seemed
to cut through the air. A queer sound—not from the
sea, not from the rigging, not from Kaare's labored
breathing at my side. It grew steadily louder. I slowly
rose, looked up.

"Plane!" I yelled as loud as I could.

In a second we were all three on our legs, steering
forgotten, pumping forgotten. The little spot which
was approaching from the southwest grew bigger and
bigger. Kaare took over the helm while I rigged up a
soaking-wet Union Jack befouled with oil. The Norwegian flag, which was now ragged and filthy, but
which we had hauled down before the worst weather
struck, went to the masthead.

"He *must* see us—he *must* see us—he *must* see us!"

I went round and got everything ready in a desperate hurry, at the same time praying aloud. Kaare
just sat and stared at the slowly growing spot high
up in the sky. Rolf stood clinging tightly to the mast.

I held the last rocket we had left. The semaphore
flags lay beside me on the deck. Kaare sat with pencil
and paper ready, dry paper from the only container
which had kept the water out. A few breathless
seconds passed. The two-engined plane grew bigger
and bigger. As it drew nearer, I lighted the rocket
with a cigarette lighter; it hissed up and burst. The
red light sank down slowly and went out. At the same
moment the plane swung sharply and came roaring
down over the *Haabet*—it had seen us!

Rolf danced around the mast like a madman. Kaare sat aft holding tight to the tiller, while the tears ran down his face. I myself could hardly see through my tears.

An hour later we had three planes around us, flying over the *Haabet* mast-high. Three planes! This time there could be no doubt. We received the same instructions as before: "Will report—follow direction of planes." And I sent the same reply: "Have escaped from Norway using call sign *D* for David thank you."

Again and again plane after plane came down over us, flew close by our masthead, and continued for a short time in the same direction. There was no doubt what they meant: we were to sail in that direction. We all seemed to have come back to life. Rolf pumped and tried to sing a little Norwegian folk song, Kaare sat at the tiller just smiling, and I could hardly contain myself.

Our courage had suddenly been reborn, and in a few minutes the vessel was under full sail. It was unthinkable for a boat like the *Haabet* to sail into port with close-reefed sails! We went so fast that the foam flew and now, according to the course the planes gave us, ran half before the wind, half with the wind on our quarter. What did a little more water matter now when it was all over?

It was past four. Then Rolf, standing on the forecastle, shouted, "Smoke ahead! Ship!"

Kaare and I sprang to our feet. There! Each time the *Haabet* cut over a wave top we could see the masts of a ship; the masts rose higher and higher and finally the ship herself appeared; she was coming straight toward us. One of the three planes flew in even curves over toward the ship, and next moment swung round and made straight for us again.

At 4:45 we were about a quarter of a mile from the British destroyer. What a sight! It was almost too good to be true. I had a feeling all the time that I was dreaming, and every time I tried to share my joy with Kaare and Rolf something seemed to lodge firmly in my throat, and I could not utter a word.

We were told through a megaphone on the destroyer's bridge to come up on the lee side, and soon afterward we got hawsers aboard both fore and aft, while the crew, who lined the ship's rail gave us three ringing hurrahs.

Without a thought of military restrictions, my first question was: "What is our position?" Five minutes later the answer came: "You are twenty miles off the English coast where the Thames comes out into the Channel!"

Kaare, Rolf, and I exchanged searching looks. Could it be possible? The English Channel, where the Thames came out? It sounded completely fantastic, but when a moment later we got the position in black and white in degrees and minutes, we were convinced.

After a keg of water had been lowered to us and we had quenched our thirst for a time, the commander told us he had received orders to pick us up, but, he was sorry to say, not our craft. Again we looked at one another. Let the *Haabet* go to the bottom now?

Kaare shook his head, so did Rolf, and I made the decision unanimous. If the *Haabet* had brought us

1,150 sea miles over the North Sea, first across then down, and at last across again, surely we could manage the forty miles which remained! The food, water, and medicine we had been given had already had their effect, and we felt equal to almost anything again. Moreover, the *Haabet* was all that we possessed!

The last words shouted at us through the megaphone from the skipper were these:

"I've heard many stories about you crazy Norwegian Vikings, but it seems to me you beat them all! Good luck!"

We ourselves did not really know what we were doing just then, but our pride in being Norwegians, our pride in having won, was too great.

Two hours later we were hailed by another destroyer with orders to sail up on the lee side. This time there was no question about it: the skipper had orders from the Admiralty to pick us up, and the *Haabet* too. This time we did not have to be asked twice!

One after another we clambered up the rope ladder and on board the destroyer *H.M.S. Bedouin*, where officers and crew from the captain, James A. McCoy, down, received us with open arms. What a welcome we got! As we clambered on board, men from the destroyer were down on the *Haabet's* deck. First the mast with the Norwegian flag was hoisted on board, after which the *Haabet* was heaved up to two strong hawsers. But she was too big to be swung on deck on the davits, as had been intended, so she was made fast hanging outboard on the destroyer's side.

Half-asleep, I remembered our hiding place with the

map and lists and more than a thousand films of
German defense works, and with these in my arms I
was carried below to the first lieutenant's cabin, which
had been placed at my disposal. Kaare and Rolf had
been treated in the same way and were already in
bed, each in an officer's luxurious cabin. With hot-
water bottles above and beneath and beside me, and
after an injection of a sedative by the ship's doctor,
I fell asleep.

This was England!

I awoke eighteen hours later, stiff all over; while I
was asleep the doctor had bandaged my swollen hands.
After a bath and a prudent lunch, I went up on deck,
just in time to see the *Haabet* torn away from one of
the two strong hawsers when a big sea washed over
the destroyer's side. No one could do anything about it.

The North Sea had won at last and got a prize it
had been after for fourteen long days and nights.

H.M.S. Bedouin was now going at full speed and
right against the wind, and when a modern British
destroyer goes at full speed, it means about thirty
knots. For more than an hour before I came on deck
in time to see the end of the *Haabet*, the crew had
feared that this would happen and had tried to
strengthen the moorings. But more than this was
needed to oppose the might of the sea!

From one steel hawser hung the remains of the
propeller and shaft, torn out of the rotten bottom when
the sea was knocking our vessel to pieces. But the
Haabet had carried out her mission; she had brought
her crew through, even if they *were* wet, weary, and
swollen.

I learned from the skipper later that they in a "full-grown" destroyer had had to put into port during the gale we had weathered, and that it was the worst he had experienced in his fifteen years at sea. He had also been told that the destroyer sent out to pick us up after we had been observed by an Avro Anson just off the Scottish coast eleven days before, had been obliged to put back because of the bad weather.

The crew had also heard on the radio that two fifty-foot fishing smacks from Norway, on their way down the coast of the Shetlands with men who had escaped, had been lost in the gale.

On our way into Hull, where according to plan we were to be landed, the *Bedouin's* skipper had received counterorders, and when we came up on deck a little later the same day, we were going at full speed in a northeasterly direction. A British plane, a Bristol Blenheim bomber, had crashed into the North Sea during a reconnaissance flight on the last day of the gale. The planes which had found us were out searching for possible survivors. And now one of the planes had reported sighting a rubber dinghy a little farther north, and it was toward this that the destroyer was heading.

With the skipper we stood watching the perfect cooperation between plane and ship. The planes repeatedly dropped parachute flares to show the direction. When at last we came near enough, we could see a small yellow object dancing up and down in the heavy swell. A boat was launched and soon came back with the rubber dinghy in tow. It was a melancholy sight. Of the five men who had been in the dinghy four days before, two remained, and only one of them was alive.

Next day I had a short talk in the sick bay with the sole survivor, a red-headed Irishman. He told me how, the day they had taken off, they had encountered the tail end of the great storm, how they had run into a fog and been unable to stay aloft in the prevailing conditions.

He supposed they had got into a violent atmospheric disturbance, and before they knew anything they were hurled downward. One of the control columns had broken, and the next thing he could remember was the crash when they hit the sea. The whole crew had managed to get into the rubber dinghy, but one after another they had been flung out by the seas.

His friend who lay dead in the bottom of the dinghy when the destroyer picked them up had simply been drowned where he lay. For the last twenty-four hours they had both been too exhausted to move.

I told him about our eight days of whole gale, and he smiled, stretched out his hand, and said: "There must have been Someone holding the tiller for you in that gale!"

The destroyer received orders to go north to Edinburgh and we had to go, too. I shall never forget the days we spent on board. It was not long before the attention, medical care, and good food restored us to normal health. We were not allowed so much as to lift a chair; everything was done for us and we were waited on like noblemen.

When we landed from the destroyer in Scotland on

October 4, it was with mixed feelings. Such friends as we had made in the short time on board *H.M.S. Bedouin* would be hard to find. But before us lay England, London, and perhaps further training in Canada for the day when we should come back to strike a fresh blow for Norway's freedom.

5   The Secret Service Calls

AFTER LANDING IN ENGLAND, Kaare Moe, Rolf Gabrielsen, and I had gone to Canada to be trained as pilots
at "Little Norway," near Toronto. Rolf, the former bank
clerk, became a skilled navigator. We flew on a number of missions together and had some close calls;
our escape from death once or twice was nothing short
of a miracle.

Not so lucky was Kaare. The summer of 1941, he
was accidentally killed in a mid-air collision with another plane during a training flight. His death left
me dazed and bewildered. Nearly every day, men
with whom I ate and worked and lived failed to come
back. But this was different—in Kaare Moe I lost a
friend, a comrade, and a man whose like I have never
met anywhere. He found a temporary resting place
in the little chapel of the training camp, but his ashes
were later removed to Norway, where they now rest
in the churchyard at Ullern.

Soon after this I was sent to England with a large
Norwegian contingent, and thence to Iceland, where
I served for most of 1942 in the 330th (Norwegian)

Squadron. Toward the end of the year the squadron was transferred to Great Britain, but not as we had all dreamed and hoped it would be. The Shetlands were our destination, and we were to get four-engined Short Sunderland flying boats instead of the lighter bombing planes we had expected.

"You Norwegians have done remarkably well in your work for Coastal Command and will therefore be the first when it comes time to undertake such a difficult task as operating a Sunderland squadron out of Shetland!" is the way it was put to us in a letter from Coastal Command.

We were certainly coming nearer to Norway, but not in the way we had hoped. Again we would be fighting the treacherous North Atlantic, not the enemy we were so eager to get at with bullets and explosives. Why should all the others get the chance? Why should every other nationality fly over Norway, and not we, who knew every hollow, every mountain, every fjord in our districts?

Now, more than two years had passed since our adventurous voyage across the North Sea, and I had been waiting since early in January, 1943, for word from the British Secret Service on where I could best serve the Allied cause next. Meantime, while my future was being decided for me, I did some occasional flying with Bomber Command over Germany and Holland.

Finally the word I had been waiting for came; and my greatest wish—the wish most of us had had since leaving our native land—was about to be fulfilled! At

last I would be fighting directly for those at home
and for Norway, not over the North Atlantic in storm
and fog that obscured the results of our missions: now
the fighting was to be done in Norway itself. So,
naturally, when I was offered the assignment by the
secret service, I accepted with alacrity. Perhaps I
did not realize, or even stop to consider, what the
task involved. For the present, that did not matter.

For three-and-a-half months I was to go to school
again. Not the kind of school I had known as a child,
with ordinary school hours spent studying things we
didn't take too seriously, but school for eight, ten,
twelve hours a day.

I cannot go into detail here, but to qualify for
carrying out the plan one had to be a telegrapher with
knowledge of the latest British and American wireless
sets used in this kind of work; a meteorologist able
to send weather reports and make observations as
required by planes; and have a thorough knowledge
of what the Allies knew of the German military and
its dispositions in Norway.

As a radio operator, one had to have a number of
different code systems at his fingertips, and there were
hundreds of other details to be mastered.

During this time I made occasional flights, and the
last one landed me in a Norwegian hospital in London
after a parachute jump in which I broke both my
legs. Luckily the fracture of my left leg was comparatively slight, so that in a couple of weeks I was able
to continue my work at the school, though at first
both legs were in plaster casts.

I had to go to school each day by car, but time was a decisive factor: the task I had could not be started later than the last week in April; after that date an agent could not be dropped over Norway because the summer nights were too light. But the problem I faced was this—would a broken ankle and a cracked fibula stand a parachute jump two months later? The Englishmen smiled doubtfully every time this question was raised. Time would have to show.

By April 17 everything was ready. In broad outline, the plan and task were as follows: The Arendal-Grimstad-Lillesand-Kristiansand-Mandal area in the southeast of Norway had for a long time been one from which the Allied Supreme Command could not get adequate information, considering its importance. In February, 1943, two agents had been dropped in the Setesdal region to deal with this most important question. But later these two fellows had had a hand in sabotage efforts that started in this region and gradually spread farther south to Kristiansand, Arendal, and Mandal.

Some of the arms dumps of Mil. Org., the military branch of the Underground, had been discovered by the Germans, and a number of arrests had been made, followed by raids and road controls. More than 150 persons had been arrested in a short time, and people on farms and in towns throughout the district were in a highly nervous state.

The situation, naturally, made things difficult for the agents, who very soon had to move elsewhere. They went to Vestlandet, where, instead of continuing with their original task, they were to run a radio station out on an island and report all shipping traffic until conditions in Kristiansand improved. But here, too, they got into difficulties; the Germans pinpointed the radio station and the agents were forced to move again.

On their journey to Oslo the train stopped at Drammen as usual; the Gestapo had its agents tracking down a specific piece of sabotage—and one of the men was arrested. He was later sentenced to death three times, but each time the carrying out of the sentence was postponed at the eleventh hour; and each time the agent was subjected to fresh torture, but the Germans never got a scrap of information out of him. The liberation of Norway ultimately saved his life, and his story became one of the many miracles of the war.

A month later a couple of agents were dropped again in the same region, with much the same result, except that these men were able to carry out their assignment in another district until they were caught and shot in September, 1944.

This was the reason why I had chosen to go alone, and why I had asked to be dropped some distance from the district in which I was going to operate. The plan called for me to be dropped without any more equipment than I could cram into a pack—a radio transmitter and receiver; the necessary codes, arms, and ammunition; a suit of clothes to replace the rough outfit I should be dropped in; and a ten-day ration of food.

Ten days later, the main equipment, weighing about 1,300 pounds, was to be dropped at a prearranged place in southern Norway; in the meantime I should have made arrangements with the people from Oslo who were to work at the first radio station. This was the plan.

I had made twelve parachute jumps, so that part of the job did not worry me too much! The last item in the program was carried out in a London cellar before I left the city with another Norwegian agent, Olav P. Wickstrom, and two representatives of the British Secret Intelligence Service. This was the fitting and measuring of the parachute and harness. The pack too, which now weighed eighty-nine pounds, was fitted into a rubber covering and fastened between the harness and parachute. The whole combination formed the famous *D*-type parachute.

Late in the afternoon of April 17 we drove into the grounds of an old English country house surrounded by high walls. Everyone here was sworn to secrecy; every man or woman, from the commanding officer down to the washerwoman, was chosen with special care. The same rules applied to all personnel, both ground and flying, at the great airfield a half-hour away.

From this airfield planes took off every night on special missions, not only to Norway but to all the European countries. There were planes which dropped agents, planes which dropped equipment for resistance movements and illegal groups, planes which landed unseen on "secret airfields" in occupied territory and in Germany itself.

The Nazis had been trying frantically to locate this airfield throughout the war, but thus far they had failed miserably. From what we saw of the antiaircraft guns and defenses around this airfield, it would be difficult to achieve much by attacking it.

The house contained an extremely cosmopolitan collection of persons who were "guests of honor" in the place—agents from the various European countries. They talked together, ate together, did physical exercises together, but no one knew who any other individual was or where he was going. One could only guess from the accent with which he spoke English. No one asked questions; no one ever talked about himself.

The thing which perhaps everyone remembers best about the place, apart from the marvelous treatment received there, was the so-called "Operational Egg." Fresh eggs were at that time largely unobtainable by the English public. Only dried eggs from Canada or America were used. Yet, once in a while at suppertime, two fine fresh eggs were carefully laid on a plate before a particular person.

The person so favored, even if eggs were his favorite food, seemed suddenly to lose all taste for the tempting delicacy now actually set before him. To him the two eggs on his plate meant just one thing: it was his turn to take part in the night's operations; a reminder of this, and a last special piece of hospitality, were the "Operational Eggs."

That evening of April 17 I was to sit down in a few seconds and see two fried eggs on my plate. The rare treat did not even whet my appetite. There was too much to think about, too many still unanswered questions connected with the coming hours and days.

6 Back to Norway

It was shortly after eight o'clock, and we were sitting together in a little bungalow down at the southwestern corner of the airfield, each of us with a small glass of old English rum in his hand. Wickstrom was in full camouflaged jumping regalia: in canvas shoes with big rubber soles over a pair of worn Norwegian skiing boots, his parachute harness on, and his rubber helmet and gloves in one hand. The harness was so tight that he could not stand upright. Similarly equipped, I sat in another corner of the little room.

Two representatives of the British Secret Service were there, and the officer in command of flying operations from the airfield. There was a feeling of constraint; the other three tried keeping up a stream of conversation about anything and everything but what we were all thinking about. Wickstrom and I scarcely heard what was said.

We could hear the drone of the engines of two Halifaxes on the airfield; the mechanics were warming them up. In the intelligence room the air crews were receiving their final instructions. The weather report was bad—a strong northwesterly wind over the district where we were to be dropped.

For the third or fourth time I looked into the chamber of my revolver, saw that there was a bullet ready in the barrel, felt to make sure that the commando knife in the sleeve of my jumping outfit was there, that the parachute harness was on properly, and that the flashlight was where it ought to be.

The commanding officer rose and lifted his glass: "To the freedom of Norway and of the world—to your success!" A last handshake, and Wickstrom was driven out to one plane, I to another. We were both to be dropped alone, he in the district around Tinnsjö in Telemark, I in the Eiker Forest northwest of Drammen.

In addition to his D-type parachute, in which the pack is placed in its rubber covering over one's head, Wickstrom had five containers which were also to be dropped by parachute. A reception committee would be awaiting him on the spot. It was the last time I saw Wickstrom: when he jumped, his parachute did not open, and he was killed instantly against the ice, amidst his friends on the reception committee.

The plane I was going in carried containers too, but they were to be dropped to an agent north of Skien.

One by one the engines were started and revved up, the magnetos were tested, and the plane began to taxi out toward the runway. Hydraulic brakes whined as we stopped at forty-five degrees to the runway for a final check of engines and mechanism. A green light from the control tower, "You are O.K.

for take-off" over the telephone, and then—a tremendous 6,000-horsepower roar. Our planes sped faster—faster—then we were air-borne!

"From now on you are Johansen—Karl Fredrik Johansen—and you were born on April 23, 1917! You are a woodcutter—logger it says on your passport—and you were born on a small farm north of Kongsberg. You are a member of the *Nasjonal Samling* (the Quisling collaborationist organization)—and are as simple and stupid as the rest of your family." I sat thinking aloud to kill time.

Only the dispatcher had his place with me in the middle of the plane. He was English like the rest of the crew, and had his job to attend to. And I felt no urge to unnecessary conversation. Without a word he arranged a sleeping bag on the floor and pointed to it, indicating that I could try to get a nap on the way over. But it was no use trying to sleep; the parachute harness was too uncomfortable, and the regulations advised against taking it off, because inside a darkened plane one could not be sure that he had put it back on properly.

From where I sat I could see out through a little square window. The moon had risen now and was sending a river of silver over a rough sea far below. Sitting there, I could not help thinking of that time long, long ago when three of us had floundered about for a fortnight in the North Sea in a small and leaky sailing boat, six months after the occupation of Norway, to get across to England.

It was fourteen-and-a-half days from the time we left Farsund to the happy moment when we were picked up by a destroyer down in the Channel. And tonight we would cruise in over the Norwegian coast less than three-and-a-half hours after leaving England.

Time passed slowly. Beneath us now lay a layer of cumulus clouds, grotesque cloud formations bathed in moonlight. The pilot had had to climb higher to get over a "front." I had borrowed a couple of telephones and a microphone mask, and it made me feel a little better just being able to follow what was happening from time to time.

Suddenly a message came over the intercom: "Light ahead—Norwegian coast to port!" I could feel my pulse beating more rapidly; a moment later I was sitting on the folding seat beside the captain. There—the faint shape of a broken coast line could just be glimpsed through the darkness, and behind it—snow-covered mountains in the pale moonlight.

For a few unforgettable minutes not a word was said. Gradually one mountaintop after another appeared through the darkness, and between them the dark wooded valleys could be seen dimly. It was like a fairy-tale setting.

We were all suddenly brought back to reality by a series of quick, bright flashes down on the ground, followed by bursts ahead of us to starboard which made the captain turn the plane over sharply to the left. The antiaircraft batteries were in full action, but as far as I could see the men behind them were suffering from night blindness. The puffs of smoke and bursts were a good thousand yards away from our position.

"Do you know where we are?" the captain asked the navigator.

"A mile and a quarter west of Farsund," was the reply.

A brief conversation followed, and the two agreed to try a little farther east. First a turn southward, and the antiaircraft fire quickly died away behind us. In toward the coast again, and this time things seemed to be going better. Soon the coast lay far astern; the course was set northeast.

Now and then we passed over inhabited regions. Single scattered lights began to appear; the people down there knew that this was no ordinary patrolling German plane out at that time of night. Suddenly a string of dots and dashes shone through the darkness from a little mountain farm: a string of V's. Someone had probably been practicing this letter for a long time. There was more: LONG LIVE ENGL—and then suddenly a stop. We never found out what happened to prevent completion of the dramatic message.

"Another hour to pinpoint!" I gave a start; for a good quarter-of-an-hour I had totally forgotten what was going to happen. It was a message from the navigator. "Pilot to 'Norway'—pilot to 'Norway'." It was for me this time.

I answered, and was told I had a half-hour in which to eat a bit of food and drink some coffee before it was time to get ready. I wasn't hungry, but I realized it would be sensible to have something inside me—it might be some time before my next meal. So the dispatcher and I sat and ate. He was trying to tell me something about his last operations over France, but his story came to an abrupt end, partly because of the noise of the engines, partly because he had an inattentive audience.

The pilot called up again over the intercom, this time with a message for the navigator. There seemed to be one thing that bothered them both—wind force. Every time the navigator took the drift of the plane in relation to the ground, the result gave a velocity of between thirty and thirty-five miles per hour. It was possible that the wind force was less powerful lower down, but in all probability it was twice the maximum allowed for parachute jumps. But that problem was one for the captain to worry about.

"We've just time for a last cigarette!" It was the dispatcher who suggested it, and he did not need to speak twice. We sat in silence and puffed away nervously.

Then: "Twenty minutes to target! Pilot to 'Norway'."

"O.K., Captain, go ahead." I hardly knew my voice. "Get ready—and good luck!"

Again I replied automatically: "Thanks for the trip; we'll meet again in a year or so—I hope!"

I broke off the connection, put on my rubber helmet, fastened it securely, found my gloves, and put them on.

I got up, stepped over a lot of parcels containing leaflets to be dropped on the return journey to conceal the plane's real mission, and sat down on the forward edge of two large doors in the floor. The dispatcher was busy checking over the parachute harness and hooking it onto the large rubber-covered pack which now hung in a slip arrangement right over the doors.

What was to happen now, in theory, was this. I was to jump out first. When the thirteen-foot-long straps from the harness to the pack were drawn tight, the pack would break loose and fall more or less straight out of the hole. On top of the pack the parachute itself lay packed: in this case a parachute thirty-two feet in diameter. The top of the parachute was in turn fastened to a steel wire sixteen feet long by a kind of string which would bear a weight of 225 pounds, and the steel wire was fastened to the plane.

When the jumper had gone thirteen feet out into the air, the pack would fall when the straps from the harness were drawn tight. Pack and man would then fall the length of the steel wire, and the wire would begin to draw out the parachute, which was about thirty feet long.

In other words, when the whole thing had fallen thirteen feet (straps) plus three feet (pack) plus sixteen feet (steel wire) plus thirty feet (length of parachute before opening)—about sixty feet all told— the string which fastened the parachute to the steel wire would be broken by the weight, and the parachute would open!

"Ten minutes to target!" The dispatcher leaned over from where he stood on the afteredge of the doors and passed on the captain's message to me. But by now my brain had ceased to function normally; there was just one sentence which kept repeating itself automatically: "You're going out through that hole!"

Then the dispatcher opened the doors. An icy blast blew up through the hole—and ran still colder down my back. There, far below, lay Old Mother Norway— mountain on mountain, valley on valley—jagged, repellent, cold! Seconds seemed like hours as I sat with my legs halfway over the hole, ready to jump.

The pilot had gone to a lower level. The Halifax heaved itself violently over the mountaintops. I tried to find a clue in the terrain, some place I had seen before, but it was too dark. Only the contours of rivers, mountains, and valleys could be distinguished against the deep blackness.

I looked back to the dispatcher's face, for I was to get my signal from him and from green and red lights in two small lamps in the roof. He was standing with the microphone mask over his face, and from his movements I could see that he was talking to the captain. The plane was swinging steadily—rising a little, then sinking again: something was not as it should be—something was decidedly wrong.

It was the wind force. In the last minutes over the hole I had sat and wondered how in the world the thing was to come off: the plane was being heaved up and down so erratically that it was hard to stay in the right place. The dispatcher found the headphones I had used earlier on the trip, and signaled to me to take off my rubber helmet. There was a thirty-five mile wind force, and the captain told me curtly that he refused to let me go.

So it was all to be for nothing—all the anxious seconds and minutes that to me had seemed like hours. Cursing fate, I wrenched off the parachute harness, crept into the sleeping bag, and did not awake till we had landed on the airfield in England five hours later.

We tried again the next night, and again I had to accept having the jump canceled for the same reason as before; this time the wind force was nearer forty miles per hour.

It was early morning on April 20, 1943; the hour was 1:45. For the third time I was sitting at the edge of the hole in the afterpart of the Halifax. This was the last night of the full moon, the last night before the summer months, during which agents could not be dropped into Norway. In other words, this was the last chance I had of carrying out the task I had undertaken.

The plane this time had a Polish crew. I sat staring hard at the dispatcher, trying to guess his thoughts from his features. Again we circled around, again the plane was flung from side to side by a strong wind; again I sat on the edge of the open hole, undergoing the worst possible mental torture. The plane began to climb again!

There must be some limits to what a man can endure. This time it was not at a dispatcher's request, but on my own initiative, that I took off my rubber helmet for a talk with the captain on the intercom. He gave three reasons for not letting me jump: (1) There was a good thirty-mile wind force, and that was fifteen miles too much. (2) He could not find a particular stretch of open marsh which should be there according to the map; all he could find were mountains and forests everywhere. (3) He dared not go too low because of the violent gusts of wind, and he could not reduce speed to less than 160 miles, against the normal 115-120 miles, because if he did he would lose steering control in the violent air currents.

I will not report the discussion that went on for at least fifteen minutes, except to state that in the hearing of witnesses—the rest of the crew by intercom—I took the whole responsibility on myself.

I was sitting at the edge of the hole again; the time was 2:07 A.M. This time it was the dispatcher who was nervous; for me there was only one thing to do: to take the chance of things' going right, and jump.

The Halifax went lower—the contours of water, mountain, and forest grew sharper—there was a terrible lot of snow—the plane swung—went straight for a few seconds—swung again—speed was reduced slightly, and the propellers set at high pitch—we went steadily lower—I was tossed to and fro—I stared at the dispatcher—green light, and "action station" from the dispatcher, who had now raised his arm—I flung both my legs into the hole—fractions of seconds —red light.

"Go!"

I started and—was out.

The wind howled in my face. I was flung around —struck my head against something, the rear wheel of the Halifax—I saw stars—many stars—a terrific jerk —more stars—a sharp pain in my back, my head— everywhere—the night was dark—I lost consciousness.

The next thing I knew I was being jerked and tossed

about violently; it was a little while before I really
paid any attention to what was happening—and suddenly there, a few yards away against the fearful
wind, I saw the rear turret of the Halifax and the
rest of the craft silhouetted against the sky. I was
hanging from the plane!

Whether it was fear or pain that made me faint
again, I cannot say; it was probably both. I recovered
consciousness feeling that I was still hanging, that I
was being flung up and down at a furious pace—and
I fainted again.

Before I regained consciousness again, a miracle
must have happened: I was on my way to the ground
far below. I looked up instinctively: yes, the parachute was open, but only part way. It looked to me
as if some of the many silk cords extending up to the
parachute had got entangled in the material and
divided the whole "umbrella" into several sections.

I looked down—far below in the darkness lay water,
mountaintops, and forest. I could only feel that I was
falling a good deal faster than I ever had before. But
there was absolutely nothing I could do about it. Yet
there was something seriously wrong with my right
foot or leg. It was hanging all wrong in relation to
the left, almost at a right angle. I tried to lift my leg
as I hung there in the air—but the only reaction was
a stab of pain.

It was blowing hard: I was approaching a ridge
just below me—dense wood—no, I was caught again
by a violent gust, passed the top of the ridge, and
was propelled full-speed down into the valley on the
other side.

I held my breath—now for it! A bunch of big fir tops came rushing at me—there was the noise of branches breaking—something like a big bough hit me in the face—everything became still.

I had fainted again.

I don't know how long I was unconscious, but gradually I came to again. There was a strange noise in my ears, followed by a strange silence, and for a few seconds, minutes perhaps, I felt that I was dreaming —felt that I had come into a completely new world. At first I dared not move, but at last I tried. A burning pain in my back brought me back to reality, and I looked up, sideways, and down.

I had landed in the top of a tree and was hanging with my back against the trunk. Above me, a dark mass against the lighter sky, hung my pack. The fir top itself was broken off and lay across a tree next to it and beyond, while the remains of the parachute were entangled in another. What a fantastic piece of luck—so fantastic that it could hardly be true!

It did not take me long to get hold of my commando knife and cut away the parachute straps. At the same time I twisted myself around to face the trunk, and slid down through the first boughs as carefully as I could. I now understood what was wrong with my right leg; the knee had been dislocated and the whole lower part of my leg, with the foot, had been twisted ninety degrees out to one side. I could only hope nothing was broken; but I would never have believed that a knee out of joint could be so horribly painful.

I collapsed at the foot of the fir tree like a pile of

wet rags and lay there with closed eyes. I stretched out my hand, caught hold of a piece of reindeer moss, and inhaled its scent. Never, never, I vowed, would anyone make me do another parachute jump; indeed, at that moment I never wanted to see a plane again!

And yet, this was Norway: Norwegian fir and pine, Norwegian bilberry and reindeer moss. Despite the burning pain in my back and knee I could not help reveling in their familiar scent, taking long draughts of the night air. Everything was so strangely quiet; only the noise of the wind in the fir and pine tops penetrated to where I lay.

The long hours in the Halifax and the mad descent through the air now seemed like a bad dream. But every time I tried to move to a more comfortable position, the burning pain emphasized the merciless reality of the situation.

How long I lay there I do not know, but it was beginning to get cold. Frantic thoughts raced feverishly through my brain. Was this to be the end? Was the task I had so lightly undertaken to end in failure before it had even begun? Would the Polish captain of the Halifax be proved right in having held that it was madness for me to jump?

Seldom have I felt so utterly miserable and helpless as on that April night, when I lay with my knee out of joint in the midst of the Eiker Forest, in a temperature of 15 and at least a foot and a half of crusted snow.

I must have slept a little after all, for I woke shivering, and every quiver sent a knife thrust through my knee. My foot had become completely numb as it lay, apparently sprained, too. The knee was badly swollen. As I looked around me, I suddenly noticed that it was beginning to grow light. Again I tried to think with some degree of clarity. Something must be done now, and quickly.

"The first thing you do, on landing in an area occupied by the enemy, is to remove every visible trace." That is the first commandment for an agent dropped into territory held by the enemy.

I lay for some time looking up into the fir top where I had landed, and on into the next tree, where the greater part of the parachute lay caught in the branches. If the plane had been observed en route to the place where I was dropped, and the Germans sent a Storch over, it would not be hard to find the place.

Even though the parachute was camouflaged, it would be seen easily enough against the white snow underneath. And then? With my bad leg I should hardly be able to crawl many yards before the Germans were on the spot, and after that all they had to do was to follow the tracks.

If I could only slip my knee in again, there was at least a chance. But could I do it without help? Close to the stem of the tree I had landed in stood a fairly thick birch sapling. Between them they formed a sharp fork. I lay looking at this fork for some time. Was this a possibility?

How long I tried and how many times I fainted, I cannot say. I had broken a few bones in my time, but till then I had never experienced anything so infernally painful as putting a knee into joint oneself, getting leverage with a broken-off stick.

If anyone had told me it was possible, I should have refused point-blank to believe it; so, perhaps, will many who read this book. But anyone who has experienced anything like it, and been in a situation in which his life was at stake, will understand and appreciate that there are times when a man can accomplish what under ordinary circumstances would be utterly impossible.

I lay looking at the parachute in one tree and the pack in the other. Now at least I could move my leg, although the swelling had spread higher up. One thing was certain: I must climb up and get hold of the pack hanging in the treetop. Its contents formed the whole basis on which my work was to start, and without it I might just as well stay where I was. The parachute must be got down too.

I will not attempt to explain how long it took and how I did it. But when the sun rose over the ridge to eastward, I was ready to start. I had repacked the pack and, on account of its weight, had thrown out a number of small things which I decided I could do without. Among the things I kept were a combination radio transmitter and receiver, a battery vibrator, a set of code books, two revolvers with ammunition, a suit of "town clothes," and provisions for two days. These provisions were packed in a watertight half-pound can, and consisted of pressed concentrates. They were used as iron rations in all R.A.F. planes in case of a forced landing.

When I left England my pack weighed eighty-nine pounds. The weight I had kept I guessed to be about eighty pounds, an extremely heavy load for a walker with a bad leg.

The all-important question was: Where was I and in what direction should I go to reach Darbu Railway Station? How far had the plane dragged me from where I had first jumped out, and what course had it kept?

I lay down and studied the piece cut out of a map which was supposed to cover the area around "pinpoint." It was difficult to see anything, and I soon found that it was futile to try to guess any position. I must begin by going north-northeast toward the top of the ridge on which I had landed. Then, if I could only get a view of the surrounding country I might be able to fix the position fairly accurately.

It took me a good hour to reach the top of the ridge. An hour of alternate crawling and staggering, an hour to cover about five hundred yards. The whole thing seemed hopeless for a while, but the view from the top raised my spirits somewhat. Judging by the map, the position was about thirty miles northwest of where I ought to have landed. Therefore, I was a good deal nearer Darbu Railroad Station than I had supposed, but I would have to cover much more difficult ground to reach it.

I had in my pack a little pocket flask of the strongest kind of English rum, and after a good swallow I set off again, half-walking, half-crawling. In the hours that followed, I tried to keep away from all northerly slopes in order to escape the snow, which was about three feet deep there.

The hours passed, and I don't know how many times I lay down, exhausted, and thought that this time I was done for. But every time I stretched out for a little while, it grew so cold that I had to get up and start moving, to keep from freezing. The right knee was now twice as thick as the left, and after each rest, when I tried to use it again, it felt as if someone had stuck a knife through my leg.

Several times I thought of making a fire, but rejected the idea on account of the smoke. If the drop had been detected, a fire would just be inviting disaster.

The whole day passed, and night approached again. I was soaked from the waist downward from crawling over the snow-covered ground, but the upper part of my body was wet with perspiration. As long as the sun was up it was not too bad, but later in the evening it grew clear and cold—the same weather as the night before, with a strong wind.

There was no question of doing a mile an hour; I would be lucky to manage a few hundred yards. To make matters worse, I began to doubt that I was taking the right direction. It seemed impossible to make the terrain agree with the map. Where according to my calculations there should have been a rather large lake, I found a river of such dimensions that I had to make a long detour to get forward at all. Where I had expected a valley and a small stream, a good-sized lake barred the way.

It was a little past ten on that first night when I lay down to sleep under a fir. One thing was clear: that if I was not to freeze to death I must have warmth, regardless of the light and smoke a fire would create.

The fire made everything seem better, and for a good hour I lay there and dried my stockings and boots, had a change of underclothing, and ate a slab of chocolate and a few raisins. To top it off, I took a good draught of English rum. I have never been addicted to strong drink, either before or since, but I maintain that the flask of rum played a decisive part on that walk.

Hard by the fir stood an old rotten pine stump, and after a lot of trouble I managed to break off some pieces for fuel. I put all of it on the fire, wrapped myself in my raincoat, and went to sleep.

Suddenly I sat up straight. What was that? The snap of a twig!

Only half-conscious, I grabbed the revolver from the side pocket of my pack. I was so cold that my teeth chattered, and it seemed to me that an echo came from the wood around me. Were there people about?

The moon was up and it was fairly light. I strained my eyes in the direction from which the sound came. Another crack! I huddled into the darkness, lying as flat as I possibly could. Something was moving behind a large clump of dwarf birch.

I loosed the safety catch of my revolver, raised my arm cautiously, and aimed as well as I could. I lay quivering in this attitude for a few seconds. There! I was on the point of firing, when out of the swamp came an elk, calmly and placidly; he sniffed a little, then went on rooting in the snow for something to eat. The wind was blowing straight toward me from the animal, and the elk was obviously unconscious of any danger.

I collapsed, weak with relief. "You fool!" I said to myself. "You prize specimen of a fool! Yes, you're the right man to send on a secret mission to occupied Norway, when you're almost scared to death by an elk!"

"Clear off, you brute!" I shouted, and the king of the forests swung round and vanished, leaving a cloud of snow behind him, while I quaked at the sound of my own voice.

It was half-past two. The fire had gone out a long time before, and it was miserably cold. A slab of chocolate went down like lightning; just a sip at the flask, and on I went, my knee protesting loudly. North-northeast, yard by yard, hour after hour. Time and again I wanted to lie down forever—but each time I grew cold, so on I went.

It was a little after nine when I rolled down a short slope and landed with both legs completely hidden in a boghole. I lay cursing myself. Then I gave a start— Did I smell smoke? Yes, certainly—upon a hillock on the other side of the swamp lay a little wooden hut, and smoke was rising from the chimney.

People! I drew my legs in and almost screamed from the pain it caused me, crawled behind some bushes, and lay watching the hut. Imagine being able to get into a nice warm hut, perhaps have a bit of food, and find out where I really was!

Not a sound was to be heard; only the smoke told its plain story.

I lay still for twenty minutes. I had slipped off my

pack, put the revolver in my shoulder holster, and now lay counting on my buttons whether I should take the chance or not. Yes, was the final decision, things must take their course.

With the help of a couple of sticks that I used as canes, and making a violent effort, I limped the fifty yards up to the hut door and knocked. A chair scraped, and judging from what I could hear, someone suddenly became busy inside and hurried back and forth across the floor several times. All was quiet for a few seconds; then the person moved toward the door, drew a bolt inside, and slowly opened the door a few inches.

I gave a start at sight of the person who appeared in the doorway: an elderly man in full *bird* uniform, the uniform of the Quislings!

"Good—" I checked myself, but very nearly forgot the rehearsal I had gone through before I knocked. I don't know which one of us made the more grotesque figure as we stood staring at one another.

"Good morning," was my cautious opening.

"Good day," the answer came slowly.

"Wonder if I might sit down for a little while," I continued. "I had a nasty fall into a hole up on the ridge and twisted my knee, and then got soaking wet!"

The man in *bird* uniform opened the door an inch or two wider and looked me over from head to foot. "Where have you come from then?"

"If I can only sit down for a little while, I'll tell you how it all happened!" I replied.

Then, reluctantly: "You may come in."

I wasted no time accepting the invitation. The man was apparently alone, at least for the moment, and I was too weary to think what would happen if there were several more like him in the vicinity. I sank into one of the armchairs in the hut, taking a rapid look around as I did so.

One rucksack—one hat—one empty coffee cup on the table. No, there was certainly nothing to be afraid of at the moment. A fowling piece hung on the wall, but otherwise the man did not look particularly dangerous.

"Well now, tell me where you've come from!"

The man obviously meant to hold his ground, and it was exactly this question that I was best prepared to answer.

"Well, I was on my way over from Sandsvaer to Darbu, and I fell into a hole up on the ridge and twisted my knee!" And to forestall further questions in the same key, I continued at once: "I'm a forestry pupil, you see, and am going over to mark some timber for Mastebogen."

"Yes, but surely Mastebogen doesn't own any timber near Darbu?"

"No, that's quite true, but I've got to go to Darbu Station to fetch some maps, and at the same time I'm going to meet an inspector from Oslo who's coming up to look at some timber that belongs to Mastebogen. We're going down to Hakavik together and shall go in from there."

It was a good thing that I was grounded in the details of local affairs, and this last statement seemed to convince the man that I belonged to the district.

It was now my turn to ask questions. "So you're one of the sensible fellows who belong to the party?" I

began, opening my windbreaker and showing a National Socialist party badge which adorned my lapel.
The man jumped up, beaming, and held out his right
hand. "Yes, I thought as much—you're very welcome!
Heil og sael!" He ended with the greeting used by
the Quislings.

I felt like laughing out loud, but I confined myself
to a "friendly" smile. The man suddenly set about
dishing up all the good things the hut afforded. The
coffeepot was filled and put on to boil; home-baked
bread, good butter, bacon, bannocks, jam—I cannot
remember all the good food the man proudly set before
me. Real, good coffee! Three cups, one after the other,
performed miracles in a worn-out body. And while I
sat there eating and drinking, the fellow's tongue
worked like greased lightning.

I found out where I was, which was the best way to
Darbu, that only the day before he had celebrated
Hitler's birthday all by himself, that most of the people
thereabouts belonged to the cursed "*jossing* class," (a
term applied to Norwegian patriots by the Quisling
party) and so on in the same key.

I had produced my pipe, although I had no tobacco.
Then I had only to help myself! German tobacco! It
made my throat sore, but I pretended to enjoy it. Naturally the tobacco was first-class. I was just dropping
off to sleep where I sat when I was startled by a sudden
question:

"Did you hear the plane that was over here the
night before last?"

No, unfortunately I had not; I had heard people

down in Sandsvaer say there had been a British plane over in the night, but I had slept so soundly that I didn't hear a thing! Had he heard it?

"Yes, indeed I did—" And then I heard a story which emphasized the suspicion I already had that the man was not quite sane. It was a British plane that had tried to bomb his hut, he declared so vehemently that the tobacco juice from the quid he was chewing ran out of the corners of his mouth. "The plane wasn't more than thirty feet over the roof. It came twice, and I had a shot at it with my gun. I'm sure I hit it, because it didn't come back again!"

For a good two hours I sat listening, half-asleep, to his fantastic stories. He had explained to me that he preferred to live alone in the forest, so there was no danger of our being disturbed.

From things he said it became clear that I was a good deal too far west of the route I had laid down. If I tried following the ridges right up to Darbu, as I had begun, I would never get there. If, on the other hand, I could get down to the road which ran from Hakavik up to Darbu, there was at least a chance of a lift from some peasant or perhaps a wood carter.

It was nearly twelve o'clock when I started to take my leave. But with the first steps I took across the floor, my leg gave way and I fell to the floor. The man immediately started to protest my leaving. "No, no, you can't get to the village in your state! You must lie down here in the hut, and I'll go fetch two or three *bird* lads, and we'll carry you to the village!"

I did not know whether to laugh or cry: the situation

was really tragicomic. His offer sounded tempting, but there must be some limit to human stupidity. Two or three others like him might, between them, be able to think more clearly than this arch-idiot!

I struggled to my feet, out the door, and down the field, while the man stood on the hut steps protesting. Across the swamp I went, past the spot where the pack lay hidden, and up through a little gully. I wanted to be sure the fellow didn't see me retrieve the pack. It was a good five minutes before he went back into the hut and shut the door, then I was able to proceed.

The hours and the day passed as I plodded along painfully. I wasn't covering much ground, but at least I was headed in the right direction.

It was about eleven that night when I reached the northern end of a long lake. According to my reading of the map, it should be Store Oeksne, but the contours didn't agree with the map. The shape of the lake was wrong, and the ridges around it did not tally with those marked on the map.

I wish I had known then that the map of the district had not been revised in twenty years, and that the original Store Oeksne had been dammed up since my map was made. Where the map showed a serviceable cart track from the end of the lake down to the village, I did not find a trace of a road. But I decided I could not find the right spot in the dark, and began to look for a place to spend the night.

Half an hour later I was well buried in wood shavings in the loft of a comparatively new hut. For once it looked as if my fortunes had taken a better turn.

7 On to Oslo

AT FIVE NEXT MORNING I went on. My knee, which I had bound up with an elastic ankle bandage, was now stiff and more than twice as thick as the other. I don't know whether it was the exercise that did it, or whether my senses had become dulled, but I was in considerably less pain. And now I was really on my way down toward the village.

There was the Eiker, and there was the scattered village. I lay prone on a mountain ridge and enjoyed the sight. It was nearly light, and the sun was just creeping up over the crest of the ridge on the other side. It was almost unbelievably beautiful. But what was in store for me next?

At a distance all looked so smiling and gentle, but what kind of people lived in the farms down there? Were there Germans in the neighborhood? What had really happened in the nearly three years that I had been away, cut off from day-to-day developments here at home?

At eleven o'clock I reached the first fence and lay for half an hour up in a patch of wood, from which I had a good view over the farm below. It was not a big

farm, but it was well-kept, with red-painted outbuild-
ings and a white main building.

A man was chopping wood over by the shed; as I
watched, an old woman came out onto the steps and
called to him. Two boys were hammering and sawing
behind the barn. But what sort of people were these?
Should I gamble on their being patriotic Norwegians
and go down and ask for something to eat? I decided
to take the chance.

The man was taken aback when he saw me come
limping down across his field. He stood axe in hand
and stared. Only when I greeted him did he seem to
recover, and after a few words about the weather he
asked where I came from. I told the same story I had
told in the hut, and he too at first seemed unconvinced.
But soon his tongue got working and he asked for news
from Sandsvaer.

It gradually became clear from the conversation
that the man's patriotism could not be questioned.
When I asked if he had heard planes over those parts
a night or two before, he gave me a long look and
only nodded. Apparently he had his suspicions, but
he seemed satisfied with the story I had concocted. I
embroidered the story about the plane—now more than
two days old—a good deal, as is usual in the countryside. But I myself had neither seen nor heard it, so
that was to be expected.

The question of food arose of itself when the man
asked me to come in, and it appeared that the family
was going to have dinner. A truck was then carrying
wood down to Vestfossen, the farmer told me, and if it
came back for a new load later in the day, I could

have a seat on it as far as the crossroads. From there I would have to walk to Darbu Railway Station. But one never knew for sure how many journeys these woodcutters would make.

At two that afternoon no truck had shown up, and after a cordial leave-taking from the kind farmer's family, I limped on. Five miles to go along a main road —I shuddered at the thought! People I passed seemed a little taken aback at the queer apparition. Peasants in those parts were evidently accustomed to knowing the people they met on the road. True enough, I was dressed like a genuine woodcutter, and the condition of my clothes would in no way weaken this impression. But it was not hard to see that the rucksack I was carrying was too heavy, and that I was limping badly.

But people would just have to stare, and think what they liked. Only three times along the whole length of the road did I take cover at the sound of an approaching car. I must admit that the sight of the second car startled me. It was a German make and open, with eight men on the deck behind. They all wore helmets and carried rifles. It was the first time in nearly three years that I had seen them at close quarters: they hadn't changed much.

I shall never forget that main road along the Eiker Lake to Darbu. It was no use to crawl there; I must limp along as far at a time as I could. And when people passed in either direction, I had to pull myself together violently in order not to show how bad I really felt.

With my last ounce of strength I dragged myself up the slopes to the main road that ran down to Darbu

Station. Only a few hundred yards more. The train, I had learned at the farm, left about six, and just as I reached the main road it entered the station. There was no hope of catching it. I just collapsed in the ditch. This *really* left me in a bad predicament. What should I do now?

The nearest house was all that interested me—I didn't care what sort of people lived there, or what happened. I shambled into the yard, slipped off the rucksack on the steps, and knocked. An elderly woman opened the door. Could I sleep over in the barn, as I had just missed the train and was going into Drammen? I supposed there was no hotel in the place or was there? Could she help me find lodgings?

She invited me into the kitchen and asked me to sit down while she talked to her husband. I sank down onto a chair, and the women disappeared into the next room. What sort of people were these?

I had scarcely completed the thought when the strains of "God Bless Our Good King," jerky and uncertain, issued from another room, the door to which stood ajar. Someone seemed to be playing the song on a child's xylophone. The moment the woman returned, she also heard the musical notes from the other room. Without a word she shut the door, giving me at the same time a searching look.

"That's my little boy who's ill!" she explained cautiously.

I smiled and said: "It's nice to hear the tune he played."

The woman gave me another searching look. "You can sleep in the barn tonight—but you must talk to my husband when he comes in."

Then, without being asked, she put a jug of milk and a glass on the table and began to butter some bread.

The husband came into the room while I was eating, and he was, if possible, even more cautious than the woman. He asked few questions, but listened closely to the story I had to tell. This was the same story I had used before, except that I was now going on to Drammen from Darbu. But I added that even if there was a place at Darbu which received transient guests, I had reasons for not wanting to meet too many people.

We then moved into the living room, where a photograph of the royal family hung on the wall, with the Norwegian flag draped round it. I offered the farmer some English tobacco, and asked if he had heard the British plane a day or two before. He just nodded, and we did not touch on that subject again.

It was not the barn for me that night, but a warm bed. From the farmer I had learned some of the changes which had taken place in the three years I had been away, and I felt completely out of touch with things. There was another thing I noticed with alarm: in conversation I continually used English words and phrases, a habit which might prove troublesome in certain situations. But it was not so easy to avoid this after having gone to English schools for three years and associated with Englishmen every day.

In spite of my bad leg, I had covered about twenty miles in three days. Now I was too tired to think out any further plans that evening, and fell asleep at once.

The housewife woke me around seven next morning

with breakfast in bed. She did not say much, and there really wasn't much to say—conversation seemed superfluous. But in spite of her silence, I think she knew all she needed to know about me. In any case, she and her husband asked no questions and offered no protests when I thanked them for their hospitality and bade them good-by as soon as I was dressed. I'm sure they understood the reason for my haste.

The ticket office at the station opened at nine, and I wanted to be there early in order to avoid meeting too many people. I was the first man at the window when it was opened, and there was no one else in the waiting room.

"Where to?" the ticket agent asked.

"Drammen," I replied.

"Have you a travel permit?"

Travel permit? That was something I hadn't thought of, nor had any of the others over in England. It was something new. In the meantime I had caught sight of a number of posters on the walls of the waiting room. "Norwegian Youth for Norway with Quisling!" "Join Up as Front-line Fighters!" "With National Socialists for a Free Norway!"

I boiled inwardly. They had not been this brazen when I left home. Without thinking, I asked the man: "Surely I don't need a travel permit to come back to Norway!"

The man was silent for a moment. Then: "What did you say?"

I tried to correct myself: "Surely I don't need a travel permit to go back to Drammen; I came from there five days ago and no one asked me for a travel permit then!"

"That may be so, but if you'd read the papers in the last month you'd have known that the new travel regulations went into effect on the twentieth; now anyone going more than twenty miles from home must have a travel permit!"

"Regulations or no regulations—I must go to Drammen!"

"Have you a passport?" the fellow asked.

"Of course I've a passport," I replied, and produced it.

"Oh, I don't want to see it," the man continued, "I only wanted to know if you had a passport."

This fellow is too inquisitive, I thought, and the man seemed to realize that I was furious. With a placating smile he stamped first one ticket and then another, handed them both to me, and explained: "One's from Darbu to Vestfossen and the other from Vestfossen to Drammen. Regulations are made to be got around, you know!"

This man was also the telegrapher at Darbu, and there was certainly no doubt now where he stood. Nor was this the last time he was to be of help to me.

But the train to Vestfossen would not leave for almost three-quarters of an hour, and to avoid people I took my rucksack, sauntered down to the main road, and sat down by the wayside. There was little traffic that morning; only a German vehicle passed now and then. Most of them were ordinary trucks; a small sedan passed and also a five-car convoy, all going toward Kongsberg.

Then an open green car came down the road at a comparatively slow speed, and it took me a while to realize that it was a police car. In the back of it sat six

Germans in full equipment with a tarpaulin over their legs. The car stopped where I sat. Involuntarily my pulse quickened.

"Got any matches?" the soldier in front leaned out and asked in a mixture of German and Norwegian. Matches, I thought—the only ones I had were made in England, but they looked exactly like the Norwegian variety. I handed him the matches without a word.

Then I had a sudden inspiration. The car was sure to be going to Drammen. Yes, quite right, the car was going to Drammen. Could I have a lift? The commander was an *Untersturmführer,* or sergeant. It was he whom I had given the English matches. He demurred at first, but finally nodded consent. I could get in with the others on the deck behind. It was not impossible that there might be trouble on the train because I was traveling with two different tickets, so this arrangement seemed an excellent one. I heaved my rucksack up first and then climbed in myself.

That was a drive I shall never forget. Beside me sat a little elderly soldier in a green uniform, who talked quite good Norwegian—and talked it incessantly. What was I doing, where had I come from, what was my name, how old was I, where was I going, what were my political views and did I know where he could get some eggs in exchange for tobacco?

He talked all the time with a good-natured smirk on his lips. Having satisfied his curiosity about me, he began to talk about other things, and it was then that I first realized what kind of traveling companions I had chosen. For a good two days his party, along with two truck parties from Kongsberg, had been combing the woods west of Darbu for parachutes reported to have been dropped from an English plane the night of the twentieth.

I grew rigid with fear where I sat, and still more rigid when he went on to praise the style of our Norwegian rucksacks. It was the pocket in particular that was so conveniently shaped—and he demonstrated by turning and twisting the rucksack this way and that.

I puffed feverishly at my pipe, trying desperately to appear calm though never in my life had I been so frightened. Then the conversation turned to the war, and we discussed whether the invasion of England would take place this spring or would be postponed until late autumn.

When we reached Mjönday Station I wasted no time in thanking them for the lift and taking my leave. It was remarkable how much better my knee felt during the first fifty yards away from that car! But I still believe that none of those eight police soldiers had the slightest suspicion that I was the man they had been hunting in the woods. For three days they had been searching in vain for what they had in their very midst; but they were utterly sick of the whole business and did no more than what they had been ordered to do.

If the same situation had arisen after I had engaged in a month's illegal activity in Norway, I would have known better than to have asked for that lift! This was one instance in which my luck was better than my intelligence.

My train journey on to Drammen went excellently. There were many people traveling, and a good many

Germans. But no one seemed to take much interest either in me or my rucksack. Drammen Railway Station had the reputation of being a dangerous spot, so I quickly disposed of my rucksack by putting it in the travelers' cloakroom.

According to the timetable there was nothing to prevent my going straight on to Oslo, but I was anxious to avoid going anywhere, in daylight, where I was known. I had thought of taking the train on to Sandvika, and the local from there into Bestum. That meant a long wait at Drammen, and this I spent in Drammen Church, well hidden in a corner.

The train pulled out a little before six, and an hour later we were in Sandvika. It was still too light to continue my journey, so again I had to wait for an hour or two. I had planned to send the rucksack on from there as luggage, but at the ticket office I was told that luggage was not sent by the local train. I therefore had to put the sack into the cloakroom, as I had a good deal of business in Sandvika, and decided to take a later train in. I hoisted the sack up into the window, and the man behind the desk took it over.

"Beastly heavy, this thing of yours," he remarked.

I held my breath at the thought of the radio set; he looked as if he were going to drop the whole bag on the floor on the other side.

"Been collecting iron?"

"Well, what do you collect when you stay a fortnight with a grandfather who's got a country farm?"

He did not reply, and wrote out the cloakroom ticket. Eighty pounds!

At Bestum Station I handed the rucksack over to

the stationmaster personally. I knew of old that he could be trusted, and I had had confirmation of this in England.

It was with a queer feeling that I walked along the old familiar roads toward Smestad. Three years is a long time to be away, and then, when a man comes back at last to the part of the world for which he has been desperately homesick, it is not a happy home-coming to feel like a hunted, unwelcome animal that has to hide and sneak around under cover of darkness. Whenever I met people, I got busy wiping my nose or tying a shoelace; if I saw a car approaching, I turned and went in the same direction as the car.

I passed Ullern Station, Bekkefaret, Ullernchaussee, and came to the Montebello Road. I stood at the crossroads and looked up toward the white house at the top of the hill, my own home. Did my family still live there? Should I walk past the door? It was against all security regulations, but all the same——

A minute later I stood outside the door, leaning against one of the posts. It was past ten, and all was quiet. If only I could drop in for just a minute, greet my mother, who no doubt was sitting inside wondering what was happening to her son abroad—greet the rest of the family. I imagined how it would feel to creep into the good old bed up in my room, dark now behind a lowered blind. Faint streaks of light escaped from the cracks around the black-out curtains in the two rooms; the dining-room window stood open.

Then the dining-room door opened, and in the light from the sitting room inside I could plainly see my mother's figure. The telephone in the house was ringing; she hastily shut the window and closed the sliding door of the sitting room again. I felt faint as I stood there; I nearly called out, nearly ran in through the open door.

I had meant to spend the night with a clergyman's family in Smestad. They were a first-class family, and I had thought of using the son in the "office" of the Oslo section. But there was no one at home, and after a short rest under some currant bushes in the garden, I went on to Ris, where my first contact lived. Originally I had planned to investigate him before approaching him directly, as the family was probably deeply involved in illegal work already. But again I had to gamble on things' being all right.

I saw a German sentry in the green police uniform in front of the house across the street, so I went on and around Ris School to use the garden entrance from the lower road. There was another German sentry in front of the school, which was next to my contact's house, but he was obviously an ordinary soldier.

I went up through the garden slowly and cautiously. A faint light glimmered through the black-out curtains on the first floor and from a window on the second, so I knew there were people at home. But what kind of people?

I waited a little while before ringing. The German sentry stood there nonchalantly on the other side of the road. If only he would make the round of the area assigned to him everything would be much easier. But there he stood—and of course the bell was in the front of the house, and the main door too.

The kitchen door was a little better concealed; but

there was no bell. My solution, therefore, was to ring twice at the front door and then move cautiously over to the kitchen door—and hope that the right person came out. If a German opened the door at eleven-thirty at night to a person who rang the front doorbell and then showed up at the kitchen door, he would certainly be suspicious. But it had to be. I was worn-out and hungry and sick of playing hide-and-seek, so I must risk it.

Someone came and opened the front door first. Curiously enough the door was shut again at once, and the same person came through the house to the kitchen door. The short light steps could not be those of any German: they were the footsteps of Wencke Tenvig, the daughter of the house. Before she recognized me, I had slipped inside the door and shut it again. Not until I took off my hat and spectacles did she open her mouth. "You're crazy!" she said.

It was a joy to meet them again—both the daughter of the house and the shipbroker Fritjof Tenvig himself. We sat up far into the night, with food and drink and endless talk! I was given a water compress for my knee and finally went to bed in the son's room, as he was engaged in so-called "volunteer work" of his own arrangement.

It was now time for me to be getting back to work. A week after the day on which I was dropped I was to meet with a "reception committee" at a fixed spot down in southern Norway to receive a parachute drop with all the equipment for the summer's work. May 2 was the last possible day for the drop, because of the light nights and the danger of being observed. Yet, I was still in no condition to carry out the assignment.

Four days had passed already, and instead of starting right in to organize the whole thing, I had to reconcile myself to sitting at Ris for a week with my leg on a chair and my knee in a compress.

A doctor had advised me to enter a hospital for a month to have the fluid drained off; and the hospital, which I visited twice, maintained I would have a stiff leg for the rest of my life if I did not do as the doctor suggested—but time was running short, and this too had to be risked.

The nurse and the Red Cross doctor were splendid. "And what name shall we put on this gentleman's prescription and card?" they asked. They both guessed the cause of the trouble, in spite of my elaborate story; I was obviously not the only mysterious patient they had had.

The name of Hans C. Qvist, a bookseller in Oslo, had been given me in London as my first contact. Through him I was to make the necessary further connections. The password, however, proved to be questionable, and I shall not forget our first meeting. It was a good week after I reached Oslo, and till then what little activity I could attempt had been confined to the early hours of the night.

Conditions in Oslo were comparatively quiet, and there was little danger of encountering anything unexpected. There were masses of Germans everywhere; but there were also plenty of civilized people to mix with. But Oslo was my own home town, and ordinarily, in peacetime, one can hardly go for a walk without meeting some acquaintance. The time of day made a difference, of course, and I made it a practice to cycle into town about nine o'clock, when most of the "unpleasant" people would be occupied in some office or place of business.

I went up to my contact's shop by a roundabout route. I had never met the proprietor, Mr. Qvist, and had no idea what he looked like. When I went in two Germans and one Norwegian were standing by the counter looking through some books. I did not want to ask for the proprietor while they were there, so I followed their example and picked up a book.

A woman behind the counter asked if I was looking for anything in particular, and I replied "French books." I had heard that there was a shortage of French schoolbooks, so I thought it might take a little time to find what the shop contained in that line.

The Germans did not seem to find anything particularly interesting, and left in a few minutes. "The proprietor promised to try to get some French schoolbooks for me," I now explained to the woman behind the counter. "Is he in?"

No, unfortunately, he was not, and he wasn't likely to be back till about eleven. Very well, then, I told her, I should have to come again.

At a quarter-to-twelve I returned to the shop. I did not even have a chance of talking to the saleswoman, for I noticed a man standing with his back to me looking at some books—I recognized him as my old friend and form-master from the high school at Ullern.

I could not go out the way I had come in; it would arouse the suspicions of the woman behind the counter, who had already seen me. So for the next five minutes I made an intensive study of picture postcards in the farthest corner of the shop.

My form-master at last finished his business and left the shop. Yes, the proprietor had come in now; would I wait a minute, as he was on the telephone. It is incredible how many things can turn up to hinder one when time is all-important.

People came and went—and again I had to study the collection of picture postcards over in the corner. This time I was hiding from the mother of one of my closest friends, who knew both me and my family quite well. Then a man in his forties appeared in the doorway from the inner part of the shop. The saleswoman spoke to him quietly and nodded in my direction.

"Yes," I said, "it is about those French books I asked for a while ago, which you promised to try to get for me."

The bookseller looked at me coldly. "What French books?" he asked. But there were two other customers beside me at the counter, so I was unable to ask for a few words in private with him.

"Are you sure it was me you spoke to about those French books? I'm sorry, but I can't recall your face— nor having promised to get any French books for you."

Yes, I insisted, he certainly had promised to get the books for me, but it was so long ago that he might have forgotten. Mr. Qvist, still deep in thought, went over to a shelf and took down the little collection of French books which the shop had on hand just then. I had been shown the same collection twice before. Then at last I had a chance of asking him for a private conversation.

"Won't it do if we stay here?" the bookseller asked, and now his face had assumed a hard expression.

"No," I replied curtly, "haven't you an office?"

Finally he led me into his office, and there we looked at one another searchingly. I took the liberty of shutting the door to the shop. "I've a message for you," I began. "Andresen, the plumber, asked me to look in and remember him to you!"

The bookseller's expression did not change in the least.

"I'm sorry, but I don't know any plumber named Andresen, and to be quite frank, I must ask for an explanation of your behavior."

I began to feel uneasy. "That's curious—you are the proprietor of this shop, aren't you?"

Yes, he was.

"Well, then, you must know Andresen the plumber," I insisted.

But no, there was no change in the bookseller's stony face.

There was only one thing to do—use the right name of the person in England who had given me that address.

"Well, there must be some misunderstanding, and I hope you will forget the whole episode. But before I go I should like to ask if you know a man called Preben who used to come in here a good deal; or we might leave that till another time."

My last words finally broke through the bookseller's distrust. He pulled me back hastily into the office, and this time he asked me to sit down. Then, his face still impassive, he said: "After that I think I am justified in asking for an explanation of all this mystery. Who are you, where do you come from—and what do you want with me?"

It was my turn now to be a little suspicious, but I finally decided I could not have made a mistake. The bookseller was only being cautious, as he had every reason to be; and so I laid all my cards on the table. Not till next day, when the bookseller had questioned England as to my identity, did I receive the handshake I had expected when first I entered the shop.

"Uncle Hans" became our chief contact in Oslo in 1943, and did a first-rate job for us. A great many identity cards and ration cards had to be obtained, and that became his chief responsibility. I had brought a false identity card with me from England, and it was good enough for the time being; but during the summer and autumn it became increasingly clear that I would need a number of different names and professions, behind which I could take cover when necessary.

In addition to identity cards valid for Oslo and all inland districts except the frontier zones, frontier dwellers' cards for the various frontier zones had to be obtained. For this purpose the bookseller enlisted the help of a young woman employed in the police passport office, who did this job admirably.

To build up an entire organization amid conditions on which I was not fully informed was not as easy as I had thought. Most of the people capable of doing a job efficiently were already up to their necks in illegal activity elsewhere. Absolutely reliable men had to be found for the key positions, and the only chance of getting them was to turn to people I had known personally and could vouch for. But it was important that as few as possible should know the other workers, and that complicated things some.

A few carefully selected persons were now approached through the daughter of the house up at Ris. Like Wencke herself, most of them had long been engaged in Underground work, but they now had to make a choice—I would not let anyone work for me who was in other illegal organizations at the same time, for too many men and women were caught who possessed altogether too much information, with the inevitable result that hundreds were rounded up and imprisoned for most of the five years of war.

I had to have an assistant in running the radio station, but it wasn't easy to find this man. I had lined up one of my best friends before I left England; but on arriving in Oslo I found that he had narrowly escaped arrest by the Nazis and had fled to Sweden the week before.

This was a discouraging setback to my plans, for it was not easy to find a man who could stand up to the conditions we would face out in the woods. Above all, he must be a man on whom I could rely absolutely in these difficult circumstances, a man accustomed to the woods and able to adapt himself to primitive conditions; a man with common sense and strong nerves, who could handle firearms if necessary, and most important of all, who could receive and execute an order.

Further, he would have to be able to slip quietly away from his daily work without attracting attention.

Rolf Millang, who had been a member of my Scout troop before the war, was more than willing, and he came close to meeting all my requirements. He was felling timber in Nordmarka, as he was to take a degree in forestry and wanted practical experience; he was working for a considerate man who did not ask unnecessary questions.

The conditions at the shipbroker's house at Ris called for more than ordinary caution. The German Police had requisitioned the house opposite; another neighbor was a Nazi, and the school just below was packed with Germans. Nevertheless, every other evening during the time I used the house as a retreat, it was the meeting place for the editorial staff of one of the most widely circulated illegal newspapers in Oslo.

Wencke, the shipbroker's daughter, was on the staff, along with two of my best friends, the Elligers twins— Ottomar and Carl Sigurd—and one or two others whom I did not know. At 6:30 P.M. the radio was brought out of a secret room, and the printing press was running in the cellar all evening. No one but Wencke knew that I was staying there, and for the time being I didn't want anyone else to find out. I had counted on using Ottomar and Carl, but not while they were working on the paper.

One evening—the day before I was to leave—the shipbroker and I were out in the kitchen having a snack. The editorial staff had strict orders not to go anywhere in the house except the cellar and the second-floor room where the radio was usually kept, because the family was expecting a visitor from the country. The old man and I were chatting quietly so no one could hear us. Suddenly the door was thrown open by one of the twins, Ottomar.

Seldom have I seen a more surprised person! In the days before my voyage to England in 1940 we had talked, in fun, of my coming back and our carrying on the war against Norway's invaders together. Well, now that one twin had found out about my presence there, of course Carl Sigurd soon would, too.

It was an exciting experience to me to be in this hive of activity. For three years I had longed to get home to my own people, and often regretted that I had ever left; I seemed to be so far from where anything was happening. Many of us had that feeling, even though in many ways we were more in the war, in the air and on the sea, than most of the people at home.

Then, too, the result of what one did was not visible to the individual; one flew for six, perhaps sixteen, hours hunting for submarines or over a convoy far away up in the Arctic or out on the Atlantic, and often things nearly went wrong. But when one returned from an operation, the war as far as he was concerned was over for that day, and he felt outside the whole thing.

That was why I had often longed to get back to my own country, where I could be in the thick of things every day, perhaps every hour of the day.

There was one severe setback to our carefully laid plans which we would have difficulty in making good: the parachute drop of all the equipment for the summer's work, which we had failed to receive before the time ran out. Now our first chance of getting it would be in August, and the big problem was what to do in the meantime for material, clothes, and food so we could work on a fairly large scale.

Ration cards were all right, but there was not too much to be had even with a ration card in those days. I could have contacted other local organizations and obtained help from them, but was unwilling to involve in our work others who had enough to do already and were in much greater danger than my associates and I.

We would just have to do the best we could under the circumstances.

After a fortnight in Oslo, all our provisional arrangements had been made. Rolf Millang and I could not do much toward setting up an office there; but the Elligers twins, with Tenvig the shipbroker and his daughter, as well as his son Jan when he returned to Oslo, were to do so as soon as we were able to give the O.K. from Kristiansand.

Our contact on the railway had been selected for us from London. It was up to him to get us travel permits, so we had to stop at Drammen where the brother of a Norwegian captain now in London was head clerk at the station. There was no difficulty about the password this time; but we were forced to spend that night in the porters' room at Drammen Station. The travel permit had to be obtained through an official in the Central Police Station in Oslo.

The whole thing went surprisingly well, and at 12:10 next day we left Drammen by the ordinary Southern Norway train. For safety's sake, we had sent our rucksacks as luggage to avoid a possible inspection on the train. Kristiansand S. was the address on the sacks, plus two different names and street addresses, chosen more or less at random. The train was filled to overflowing, and we had to find ourselves places out in the corridor. Rolf sat on a box and I on a good-natured fellow passenger's trunk.

On our arrival at Nelaug Station we went to the refreshment stand for a couple of bottles of mineral water. As we quenched our thirst, I noticed a man who seemed to be taking a marked interest in us. When I went out for a stroll around the station he followed me.

With strong misgivings I headed for the station lavatory. The man followed me, looked to see if there were any other people about, came up to me, and said: "Regards from Drammen and I was to give you this."

He pushed a scrap of paper into my pocket and left.

As soon as he had gone I pulled out the paper and read the note.

"Don't go to Kristiansand; there is a check on all travelers into the town."

That was all, but it was more than enough for us. We had exactly three minutes to get our sacks and bicycles off the train, over the vehement protest of the porter, who could not understand why we did not know where we were going.

But what were we to do now? Our travel permit was to Kristiansand. I hardly think the stationmaster believed the reason we gave for the change in our travel plans; but "an aunt dying at Arendal" was something that might happen to anyone!

How the man who brought us the message could have known it was dangerous for us to come up against a control, how he knew our exact description, and how he received the message from Drammen so quickly remained a mystery.

From Arendal we went on by bicycle. Unfortunately, it was still too early for tourist or summer traffic, so

the sight of Rolf and me on bicycles with heavy packages aroused considerable interest among the country
people at every place we entered in search of food.

The same thing happened when we knocked at the
door of a little farm a mile or two from Lillesand,
soaking-wet after bicycling for several hours in a
downpour. We asked if we could sleep in the barn
or shed, and there was a low-toned conversation between us and the farmer's wife with the door open
about four inches. When we had explained that we
were students on vacation to get work in Setesdal, the
door was slammed shut and we thought for a moment
that we had met with a rebuff.

Then we heard someone moving slowly across the
floor inside, and this time the man of the house came
out. The whole story was repeated and there was a
few minutes' discussion, while the man had time to
look us over closely. Then at last we were given shelter—not in the barn or shed, but in a small hut a little
farther from the house itself. Had this been done in-
tentionally, to keep us as far from the house as
possible? Yes, from the man's suspicious, wrinkled
forehead there could be no doubt of that.

We were fairly comfortable in that tiny hut; from
the posters on the walls and other things around the
place there was no doubt that the family was O.K.
Evidently the son of the house was running his little
secret patrol, although the Scout movement had long
been prohibited by the Germans.

So we slept pretty well that night, much better than
we would have slept had we known that our nearest
neighbor was one of the leading Nazis in that area!

8   The Upturned Boat

Up in Tveit and Birkenes all was quiet. Rolf Millang, in addition to a good deal of other preparatory work, had taken a job as farm boy with the Aabels, thereby considerably strengthening our position as "students." Now it was full steam ahead again; the station was to be moved, and we could start to work on a broader basis.

The countryside around Kristiansand had long ago been combed in every direction to find the best position for a station. It ought to be in a place which afforded an unimpeded view of the whole port of Kristiansand, so that along with situation reports we could send the exact time of ships' arrivals and departures. But at the same time the station would have to be so situated that there was little chance of its being quickly discovered: in other words, it had to be somewhere off the beaten path.

There was another very important factor to be considered: it must not be too far away. Each battery or accumulator, full, weighed nearly sixty pounds. These would have to be carried up to the station from wherever we could get them charged. Along the high road this could be done on a bicycle, but they would have to be carried through the woods on a man's back.

And naturally, this time we were not going to place the station right under the noses of the Germans. After carefully surveying Kristiansand -and the surrounding district, we chose the "Upturned Boat" as the best place for our station. It was the highest point in the vicinity, only about three miles outside Kristiansand along the road on the Södal side. It was a summit about 750 feet high, rising straight from the road and shaped like an upturned boat. It was a hard job to get up the steep grade, but its various "shady sides" far outweighed its disadvantages.

We spent several days in a row carefully studying the "Upturned Boat" and the surrounding area. There was not much sense in moving the whole apparatus up to this new place, if there was any danger that we would be compelled to move again a few days later. We found the place for the camp above a little marsh thickly covered with birch trees, on the farther side of the actual top.

A path ran across the bog and continued down the precipitous side of the ridge to the road in the valley. But the path had obviously been originally trodden out many years before and was now little used.

On the edge of the marsh stood the remains of an old shanty and beside it the foundations of another house. The shanty had collapsed, but a large part of the roof was still intact. Before any of the technical equipment was moved up, we built a little shelter for the radio station up on the rocky slope, on a ledge above the bog. The place was fairly inaccessible and well covered on all sides by leaf trees. We ourselves set up quarters in a tent a little farther along the same ledge.

There were two things about the position of the station which we did not like. About a hundred yards below the top of the "Upturned Boat" and south of it began the German area which had formerly been part of the shooting range. About a mile and a quarter north of our own radio station, the Germans were installing a new main station for Kristiansand. In other words, we would have to use utmost care twenty-four hours a day to avoid being detected from these two places by Germans picking berries, going for evening walks, or doing errands.

The only place we could get the accumulators charged proved to be, after many vain efforts elsewhere, at the house of our contact Arne. Among the things sent from Sweden were a charging transformer and an oxygen meter, so this part of the job was in order. But to have a six-volt accumulator buzzing down in the cellar was far from safe; yet the whole family co-operated splendidly and continued to do so through much unpleasantness later in the summer of 1943.

Messages began to stream out from the radio station up at the "Upturned Boat." We kept watch at our lookout post every morning from before light till about 11:00 A.M. In the afternoon we were on watch from five o'clock until dark.

In this way we could observe all shipping that used Kristiansand, and the Allied Supreme Command usually knew the most important details about an hour later. Kristiansand was of strategic importance because, as the Germans' chief naval base and port in southern Norway, all the convoys which were to go south, west, and north along the coast of Norway with supplies were formed there. In the harbor, too, all the convoys for the voyage to Denmark were given escorts; and convoys coming from the west also usually came into Kristiansand.

Along with the reports from our direct observation, details concerning the same ships, sent up from our contacts in town, were sometimes telegraphed. As soon as the British were informed of the number of ships, their size and escort, what time they had weighed anchor, and their speed and course, they could decide whether it was worth while to make an attack immediately, or wait till they had got the whole convoy further along the coast.

From the reports we sent out they could easily calculate where the convoy would be at any time, and could deliver attacks with astonishingly good results.

In fine weather, we had a view from the "Upturned Boat" right over to Mandal in the west and to Grimstad and Arendal in the east. With such a view, we were able to send the position reports on convoys within an hour after they had sailed.

But the "Upturned Boat" was unfortunately something of a paradise for people who were fond of woodland and open country. We thus had a good many visitors, and on a Sunday as many as fifteen or twenty people showed up at our lookout. At these times we had to go for a walk, too; we would take a little rucksack with some food in it and sit down on top of the summit.

That we disappeared from the place several times a day and came back again a little later did not seem to arouse any undue interest. As long as they were Norwegians we did not take these visitors very seriously, but quite often Germans in uniform or in civilian clothes came up to admire the beauties of nature, and these visitors we did not much care for.

We gradually built up a very nice little station. We helped ourselves to "building materials" every Sunday from the German radio station nearby. As a rule there was no one there on Sunday, except a sentry who was usually sound asleep.

One thing became clear very quickly—that two men could not carry on this work alone and at the same time run it at all securely. Now and again, for a few days at a time, we might get a little help from one of our contacts in the town, but that was not nearly enough.

When one of us was in town gathering reports, food, or equipment, and the man who had stayed behind had to leave the station for the lookout post, we had no guarantee that some unauthorized person would not inadvertently stumble upon the station itself and the camp. The person in question, if he happened to be a Nazi or a Nazi sympathizer, could go quietly to the nearest farm and call up the German Police, and on our return we would walk right into the enemy's arms.

I telegraphed to England. The man with whom I had planned to co-operate before I first left England must now, I said, be sitting in Sweden, horribly bored. Why not send him back? Our suggestion was quickly approved, and we were told we might expect Hjelm Basberg in a month's time; further information would be sent to us.

We therefore had only to try to keep the station

fully active until then, but this was easier said than done. The Germans knew perfectly well that there must be a secret radio station in the immediate vicinity of Kristiansand. Time after time convoys left the port; time after time they were attacked in practically the same place, where there was neither harbor nor shelter for a ship that became a casualty. Ship after ship was sunk; cargo after cargo failed to arrive at its destination.

Their efforts to find those responsible were visible to us from time to time. Direction-finding planes were now very freely used; another had been flown to Kjevik to take part in these efforts. There were days during our contact when we had to lie flat in the heather up on the "Upturned Boat"; there were times when we were convinced that a plane had found the station. It would circle around the top four times, flying low; from where we lay behind a bush we could plainly see two men on board searching every square yard with binoculars.

Once when it seemed that the Fiesler Storch had received our signals on its apparatus before taking off from the airfield, and had probably made a provisional direction-finding, we had the chance of trying a new system. The word, "Plane!" from Rolf, who was keeping watch above the station itself, followed by, "It's making straight for us!" made me jump.

I did not send "wait" this time, but continued my signals, though suddenly reduced in strength. The result was evident immediately; the Storch turned abruptly, flew several times around the place where the signals had suddenly become weaker, and then returned on an exactly opposite course.

I raised the signals slowly to maximum strength; the plane turned about again and started afresh. Then I sent the single word "wait," and after that I had to discontinue contact for a long time because the Storch would not abandon the search.

But it was not only planes that interfered with our activities. There was a control on all roads into the town. These controls were tiresome and annoying, especially when one had an accumulator on his luggage carrier. That no one was caught by these controls was due more to the incredible stupidity of the Germans than to any cleverness on our part.

Because of the controls, it became necessary sometimes to send people ahead when something "dangerous" was to be transported. This gave us at least a chance of finding out what lay ahead of us and we could act accordingly. But when a motorcar patrol came along, or some other mobile form of control, there was nothing we could do before we were right up against it.

The farmer at whose house we kept our bicycles while running the station at the "Upturned Boat" was said to be trustworthy, but we were never quite sure of this. We were out on the moor picking berries, we said, but anyone must have been able to see, for example, that the biscuit tins we used for carrying accumulators were heavier, or at least just as heavy, when we went up onto the moor after a visit to the town.

That twelve or fifteen Germans were busy every day carrying loads to their radio station, a few hundred yards farther along the road, did not make it any easier for us to operate *our* station without being detected.

9 The Poacher

AFTER FOUR GOOD-SIZED SHIPS in westbound convoys had been sunk in the course of a week, things suddenly became lively in the countryside around the "Upturned Boat." As far as we could discover, the Germans were now sending a number of patrols of mountain troops out into the area every time a convoy of any size was to leave Kristiansand.

It became virtually hopeless trying to run the station so long as there were only the two of us. We were on our feet as much as twenty hours a day, for to sleep while it was light could easily have disastrous consequences.

But fortunately the end of July was approaching, and if we could hold out for the rest of that month, conditions were bound to improve.

Then, around four-thirty on a Friday morning, we were both on the lookout on top of the "Upturned Boat." We counted the ships with the aid of our binoculars: eight cargo boats over and nine under 4,000 tons. In other words it was pretty certain that a large convoy was to sail westward. We had already, a few hours earlier, sent an advance report based on observations made the evening before.

And there they went out slowly, one by one, between Odderoen and the antisubmarine defense outside. The escort was coming from Marvika in the Toppdalsfjord. Rolf sat and wrote while I peered through the glasses and described each ship's size and appearance.

In our absorption we did not notice that we were not quite alone. It was not till the last ship had left the harbor and we had half an hour before the next contact time, that I decided to run up to the camp and get the telegram coded and sent. Then I noticed something moving behind some trees on a hillock about 350 yards away. As I rose, something white disappeared behind a thick fir tree.

I went on as if I had not noticed anything, but I whispered to Rolf, "There are people about—just go on as if nothing has happened!"

I sauntered very slowly in a direction opposite that where the white object had moved, entered the wood, and then ran up at full speed.

I looked around carefully—there was not a trace, not a sign of life. For a good half-hour I sat quite still above the place, but still there was not a sound to be heard, except the usual concert of birds hailing the sunrise.

I was puzzled. Had I been as badly mistaken as all that? Was I that sleepy, or were my nerves really beginning to give way? It could hardly have been an animal, or perhaps—no, I had seen a face quite plainly through the firs.

We would have to miss contact and send the most important news two hours later. But to be on the safe

side I took a long exploratory walk before we made
our way back to the station.

The whole day passed without our hearing or seeing
anyone. The traffic on the road, 750 feet below the
lookout post, was going along as usual—perhaps a little
busier than usual. But although everything looked
quite normal, we were distinctly uneasy; we felt that
someone was watching all our movements as soon as
we were outside the camp.

It was about two o'clock when a twig snapped a
short way below the marsh. We had just eaten a slice
of bread each, and were going to try to take turns
sleeping. We both started up—someone was coming
up the path!

In a twinkling I had the sack containing the "holy of
holies" fastened on my back—all the code books, the
crystal set we were using, and the detailed plans for
running the station. And there we lay, each on one
side of the way up to the little shelf with a good view
down onto the marsh, ready for whatever might be
coming up. If there were many of them, we wouldn't
have a chance.

A man was breaking through the undergrowth on
the lower side of the marsh—a man in civilian clothes.
He was a Norwegian and, judging by his clothes, one
of the local peasants. He went on slowly up the narrow
gully toward the "Boat" and passed the top a scant
ten yards from where we lay.

I think we both had the same thought: how lucky
that during the time we had lived on that ledge we
had been careful not to make any tracks in the grass

which a snooper could have followed to our retreat. We had jumped from stone to stone behind thick wild-raspberry bushes close to the rock wall; even down at the brook we had always taken water at different places.

Again we kept watch at the lookout post in the evening; again a number of ships of different sizes assembled in the harbor, probably to sail the next morning; and again an advance report of the number of ships went by radio to the Allied Supreme Command.

At a quarter past three next morning we were both again at the lookout post. It was still dark, with just a suggestion of daylight over the mountaintops to the northeast. It was cold. Over on the marsh east of the summit, a belated blackcock was calling. The sky was clear and still strewn with stars.

Suddenly, the blackcock's calling was silenced; there was a snapping of dry twigs as it rose and flew off northward. We had both noticed this, but had little time for further reflection. We heard anchor chains rattling and steam winches working; for some reason the ships down in the harbor were taking off early that day.

I sat straining my eyes through the binoculars; it was almost hopeless to try to distinguish details—I could barely make out the number as they passed out. Rolf made notes and tried with the naked eye to determine which ships they were according to the notes we had made the evening before.

Then we both started—a twig snapped somewhere down in the direction of the German area. I lowered my glasses slowly. "Don't show you've noticed anything!" I whispered. Rolf just nodded in reply. Then I said aloud, "It's beginning to get light—we'll soon have to see about picking some berries!"

Humming the Nazis' *Horst Wessel* song, with my hands in my pockets, I sauntered down toward the spot from which I thought the sound had come. But there was nothing to be seen, and everything was quiet—oppressively so. Back I went over the fence which marked off the German area and up to the top. Rolf was sitting with his back against a stone humming to himself. "Not a thing!" I whispered.

Again we thought that we had deceived ourselves, but to be on the safe side we remained hidden where we were, glancing now and again toward the harbor, where the details were becoming clearer. The convoy of twenty-two ships was proceeding westward—if only we could get our report off!

We remained where we were, looking cautiously down toward the German area. I was whistling aloud when Rolf's leg moved slowly toward mine and gave me a gentle kick. "There! Look there! Toward the big fir by the stone a little way inside the fence!" Rolf whispered; he found it hard to control his voice.

"I'll go down and have a talk with him," I whispered back. "Perhaps he's only a Norwegian. If there's trouble try to get behind the man—if there are many of them, go cautiously up to the station—take the 'holy of holies,' warn the boys, and clear off to Oslo—get the news over to England!"

I loafed across into the German area with my hands in my pockets. The white of the man's face was visible through the bushes behind which he was standing.

"Is there any reason for playing hide-and-seek so early in the morning?" I called to him. "Is your watch right?"

There was no need to shout; the man was standing hardly ten yards away. When I received no reply, I went on a few steps, and suddenly went hot with fear when I realized that I had neither passport nor revolver on me—only a stout birch stick.

Then at last the man sprang out and shouted, "Halt!"

I trembled. So after all it was a German.

"Hands up!" He did not say the words, he hissed them.

I stood still with my hands in my pockets.

"Hands up!" he repeated loudly, and pointed his rifle at me.

I racked my brains trying desperately to decide what to do next. Was he alone, or was he yelling so loudly to attract the attention of others close by? He yelled once more, and this time I thought the rifle would go off. Only a gigantic bluff could save the situation now. I continued to stand still with my hands in my pockets, and just stared the man in the face. At last I answered in German as calmly as I could:

"But, sir, this is a queer way to greet a friend so early in the morning—a very unpleasant way! I ask you politely what the time is—and get a rifle pointed at me by way of reply!"

He became still more furious, if possible, and demanded: "Your passport!"

"What right have you to ask for anything of the kind? I'd like to see your papers first! I don't walk about in the woods at this time of day with timber cargo in my pockets. If you want to see papers, you must come with me down to the farm where we're staying now."

The man went on, scarlet with anger: "Three mornings in a row I've stood and watched you up there; you've spied on the harbor with glasses, noted the ships leaving, and disappeared as soon as they've all gone! Give me an explanation—why are you up here early every morning?"

I tried to smile as I replied: "In the first place, we've not been spying, even if your idea is quite a good one. Glasses are necessary to see that poachers like you don't shoot game. And as to taking notes, may I tell you that my friend writes poetry? By the way, sir, would you mind not talking so loudly—I'm not deaf!"

My part of the conversation was carried on in very bad German, but there was no doubt that the man understood what I said. "Hands up!" he yelled again, "and come down to the guardroom with me. We'll soon settle that part of the business!"

He emphasized his words with a threatening movement of his rifle.

My only chance now was a bluff. I glanced over the shoulder of the man, who was fuming with rage. I stood for a moment looking across toward some trees in the background, smiled openly, nodded several times, and turned to the German again:

"I don't think so—it would most certainly be very unhealthy—perhaps for me—perhaps for you!"

The man, who was about forty and thickset but small, fell straight into the trap. "Where's the man who's with you?"

"Men, you mean," I replied. "There are six of us keeping watch up here now—and three of them are in the woods behind you at this very moment!"

The German was clearly confused and frightened. This was the only chance for me now. I nodded toward the bushes in the background again. The man's voice had suddenly begun to quaver; he grunted something incomprehensible, but he did not dare turn around.

With my hands still in my pockets, I slowly turned my back on him. "Good morning!" I said, and went as calmly as I could up toward the top of the "Boat." I expected the shot every moment, and admit that I was trembling with nervousness. But there was not a sound—not a shot—not a word.

Over the top and down the other side I scrambled. At the same moment Rolf came crawling out from behind a rock. At the critical moment he had flung a stone into the bushes behind the spot where we had stood, and the noise had given me the idea—although for a moment I thought there were more Germans on the way up. Now the only thing was to put the best face on a bad situation; we walked openly as if nothing had happened, and sat down for a few minutes on a large rock.

For safety's sake I shouted the names of one or two fictitious people, received no reply, and remarked in a loud voice that the others had probably gone for a walk.

The German had followed us and was sitting on a rock a little lower down, probably to show that he was not afraid. "Let's go down to the village and get some milk!" Rolf proposed, so loudly that the German could not help hearing it. "Good," I replied, and we started down together—the German some distance behind.

"The devil!" Of course we could dispose of him, but what would the result be? Shooting which undoubtedly would be heard; the German would be missed when the guard paraded at eight o'clock; the countryside would be gone over with a fine-tooth comb; extra controls would be put on all roads. No, this was a case in which one's personal desires must be kept in check and reason allowed to prevail.

On the edge of the steep drop down to the valley the German gave up. We had passed within a few feet of the ledge with the radio station; everything was peaceful there. Halfway down the hillside we stopped and listened; all was quiet. At the farm we took our bicycles and went up the valley. Behind the first bend and well covered by the woods, we left the road again, hid our bicycles, and proceeded up the slope.

Not till three hours later, having combed the country between the German radio station and our own to be sure that our retreat was clear, did we slip cautiously down the rock wall to our camp. The report on the convoy which had sailed that morning was sent off in record time, together with a message that we were closing the station for a few days—because of "disturbances."

With all our equipment except the accumulator, we went back the same way, and then into town on our bicycles, with all the stuff behind us. As a precaution we started back fifteen minutes apart, in case of control. We met again farther on, and continued toward town with Rolf fifty yards behind, out of consideration for the "holy of holies" which was hanging upon his chest. If I were stopped, he at least would have some chance of getting away.

But all went well—we went through back streets of Lund over to the Sörland Road, deposited our sacks in Oddernes Churchyard, and for safety's sake cycled up Kongsgaard Allé to Volle Lake to have a look at the general situation.

10   Coming Tonight

It was eight that evening when, worn and tired, we came into the Aabels' farmyard. Yes, there was room in the loft, and we were welcome to sleep there. If we had come with fifty men, I think the answer would still have been the same. That night we ate a decent meal for the first time in two months, and later we enlightened the two men of the family to some extent about ourselves—that is, we told them frankly that we were not really students and were not hanging about the roads for amusement.

I don't think this was exactly news to them; they had long before put two and two together and got a pretty accurate idea of what we were up to. But they were astonished when, from the bicycle bag which they themselves had handled on several occasions, we produced the radio. In a few minutes news came from London.

"Four German cargo boats out of a convoy of twenty-two were sunk this morning by British torpedo planes off the southwestern coast of Norway. The aggregate tonnage of the vessels was about twenty thousand. One plane did not return."

I just held out my hand to Rolf and smiled. "We'll

get there some day!" Counting the four ships sunk that day, there were fourteen notches in our birch stick.

We were also cheered by the fact that the time for the parachute drop with the supplies we had been dreaming of all summer was drawing near. Because of its many advantages, a spot in the Svaland Moor was chosen, a place about three miles west of the Sörland Road at Aabel. We knew the ground thoroughly from our stay in the hut at Birkenes. We still wanted to be able to use this hut, and as usual Jörgen Birkenes had no objection to this.

But there was another hut which was now more important to us while we were waiting for the drop by parachute: Rugsland's hut, which lay on the edge of the marsh where we meant to receive the drop. There were no difficulties about this either, and next day the necessary equipment was moved up.

On August 12, Hjelm Basberg arrived from Stockholm. He had been delayed on the journey from Sweden because of steadily increasing difficulties on the frontier and in Oslo, but all had gone well just the same. It was three years since I had seen him, but he was not much changed. Hjelm was a fellow who knew what he was about, a woodsman who knew the conditions better perhaps than most, and who, above all, had complete control of his nerves and was sure-handed if it came to shooting.

The day after Basberg's arrival we received this telegram: "Coming tonight. Keep watch at time agreed. Seven parachutes and one separate parcel."

There was feverish activity that evening. We had planned every detail in advance; a cave halfway down a rock wall nearly a hundred feet high, three-quarters of a mile below "pinpoint," had been chosen as a dump for the most important things dropped. Everything, too, which had any connection with our radio activities was hidden on the ledge.

The place was very inaccessible, and anyone who did not know it well would have to use a rope to get down to it. It was impossible to see the ledge and cave from above; nor could they be seen from other directions. A carefully thought-out plan of retreat was decided on in case anything unexpected should happen.

We had made an agreement with Nils Daland, the schoolmaster, who lived in Birkenes and had been brought into our circle, that he should give us a hand with the actual drop. Thus there were four of us waiting at twelve o'clock. It was a clear starry night without a cloud in the sky; there would be a full moon in two days.

The wind was blowing from the north, between ten and fifteen miles an hour, and it was cold. Out on the marsh were pegs with white labels, marking the places where the different men were to stand, each holding his light so as to form a triangle for the pilot. In addition to the flashlights, we had fixed up two cans containing shavings soaked in kerosene.

The minutes passed slowly. Now and again I took a short walk up to a hillock above the marsh, partly to check the direction of the wind, partly to listen. But all was quiet. Twice I thought I heard the sound of planes farther south, but I must have imagined it.

One o'clock came. Still all quiet. Half-past one: not a sound. The wind had increased in strength and shifted a little to the northwest, so that we had to change the direction of the triangle a few degrees. I didn't much like this turn of events; in the first place, it would be harder for the pilot to estimate the wind and therewith the actual drop; also, with the direction of the wind the plane would fly low over the only farm in the district—a farm occupied by Quislings. But it was now or never!

It was nine minutes to two. I sat on the little hillock and listened, dozing off once for a moment or two. Then I gave a start—the sound of a plane! Yes, there was no doubt this time—but was it the plane we were waiting for?

Yes! I bounded down to the marsh, where my companions already had heard the noise. All stood ready, flashlights in hand; there it came, a four-engined Halifax! What a sight—it looked like a black ghostly bird against the paler starry sky.

A loud whisper from me, "Light!"—and three beams from well-shaded lights were flung up toward the plane. One circle—run in—there! One parachute after another, like pearls on a string—one, two, three, four, five, six—and seven! But what about the parcel? The plane swung around and came back, but turned away sharply in the middle of its run in.

What had happened? Why didn't the fellow clear off as fast as he could? There he was coming in again—but again he turned away.

"All lights out!" I shouted furiously. That pilot was bound to wake half the people in the neighborhood before he went off!

At last he himself had evidently made the same discovery. The plane vanished to the northwest like a black shadow.

Unfortunately the wind had caught the parachutes and carried them southward at high speed. We found them about two hundred yards from the triangle. It was dark inside the wood, but the parachutes, all of them entangled in boughs of good-sized trees, stood out in dark silhouette against the sky. Every man worked in silence; this was a business that must be done quickly. If the parachute drop had been observed, it was hard to say how soon a visit might be expected. Nor could one thousand pounds and more be unpacked in a short time.

It was 4:00 A.M. before all the hardest work had been done. Till then all had been quiet. Each container had in it three tin boxes, in which the gear was packed; the most important, which held new sets of code books, radio equipment, and new crystals, was marked with a large white X, and these things were the first to be placed in the cave.

As a safety measure the Schoolmaster Daland was now sent home. In case of a "visit" it was arranged that he should send a message to us by his brother-in-law Aamund.

By 8:00 A.M. all the most important items had been distributed; everything of technical importance had been stowed in the cave, while all food, clothing, and other things of a personal nature were scattered in a number of different hiding places well covered by fir branches.

Among the things dropped were 270 pounds of chocolate, 5,000 cigarettes, tobacco, canned meat, dried plums, apricots, and apples, and many other things we had dreamed of for months. Although we were all dead-tired, we were in the highest spirits. How much chocolate each of us ate during those hours, and how many cigarettes we smoked, I cannot say, but it was a wonder none of us got sick.

For safety's sake we took a bundle containing chocolate and some cigarettes, and laid it on the ledge along with the most important things. After this we all took sleeping bags and lay down in the heather on top of the cliff. All the automatic weapons and ammunition which had been dropped were also stored on the ledge. In the event of trouble, it would be a question of who was quickest on his feet.

Rolf and I were the first to try to get a little sleep, with Basberg on guard. We lay in our sleeping bags fully dressed; we had taken off only our boots.

It was 9:30 A.M. and we had been asleep for a half-hour. Actually, I had been only half-asleep, and the moment Hjelm touched my shoulder I was wide-awake. Hjelm did not say a word, only handed me the glasses and pointed; he was lying doubled up and hardly moved.

I lay where I was without changing position, took the glasses, and there, straight across the valley on the other side of the brook and at about our own elevation, only two hundred yards away, stood a German gazing across to where we lay. Mountain troops!

He probably saw us at about the same moment I saw him. A few seconds later, a bullet came smack against the rock wall between Hjelm and myself—a miss by inches only. Another—and another! We lay flat for a moment, while the bullets pattered against the rock above us.

Rolf was sleeping as soundly as ever. I wriggled up to him and shook him awake; I forced his head down when he tried to raise himself, and quickly apprised him of the situation.

"Put your boots on quick—we're spotted!"

I have seldom met anyone who can sleep like Rolf at any time, even if the situation is critical and his life hangs by a thread. "When I count three we go, and you follow five yards behind!" I gave the same orders to both men.

"Three!" As we sprang to our feet we saw behind us a little higher up and about twenty yards away, a whole party of these green-clad devils! When they first saw us, it seemed that for one precious moment they did not believe their own eyes: in any case there was perfect quiet for a few seconds. Then came a hail of fire from machine guns and rifles, but we hardly noticed the bullets singing around our ears; one thought only possessed us: "Keep ahead! Run for your life!"

Off we went along the route we had planned in advance in case anything went wrong: down a steep mountain cleft to the sheer drop—a jump into the top of a fir growing close to the wall—full speed one after another through the fir branches to the bottom of the valley.

There we gave them the slip for the first time; the Germans evidently didn't dare to jump, but went the long way around. The German who had first detected us, however, had made for the same valley bottom, probably following the direction of the firing. He came crashing down through the undergrowth twenty or thirty yards above the tree just as we reached the ground.

The three of us running for our lives will never forget that hunt, which went on for hours in every direction across the moors. Down cliffs and up slopes, over pools and brooks, now lying flat on our stomachs, now in a wild chase under a rain of lead.

It soon became clear that we had to deal not with a few small patrols, but with several hundred men posted over a widespread area. Now we realized for the first time why we had been undisturbed for such a long time after the actual drop.

We had been running for a good three hours, and still had some of our pursuers close behind us. We tried by every means we could think of to shake them off, but without result. By now we were pretty well exhausted. For the second time we were crossing the same great bog southwest of Gullringstjern, and had gained on our pursuers over the last ridge and down the cliff.

We were following the same track we had made the first time and which the Germans had now turned into a broad street. But instead of continuing up the valley on the other side, as we had done the first time, we turned back at a sharp angle along the edge, walking on stones all the time to avoid leaving tracks. Until we could hear the leading pursuer grinding up the slope to the bog, we followed the edge, then made a sharp turn into a narrow little cleft and flung ourselves down behind a large rock.

We gasped for breath and lay still: we dared not even hope to escape. There came the first man; he stopped for a moment, visibly tired, and then made off across the bog along the same track which we had followed. It worked—he disappeared at a dangerous speed up the valley on the other side. For a moment we thought of firing, but realized at once that it would be madness. There they came, more of them—they also followed the track and disappeared up the valley.

Four men so far—obviously four men in good physical condition and well-accustomed to Norwegian forest country. Had we eluded them? For the time being at any rate. We lay still for some minutes, hardly daring to move. If only we could get over to Trolldalen, we would stand a chance. It was not far as distance is measured, but how many posts and patrols had the Germans stationed between us and that valley?

Revolvers in our hands, we crawled up the mountain cleft. The rule we had agreed on in advance still held good, and we repeated it anew to one another: If one of us was wounded, it was the duty of the others to finish him off. Not only were our own lives at stake, but each of us was responsible for many families and individuals apart from the many secrets of the work we were doing. If one of us was captured, no one could know what might happen to all these people and these secrets; perhaps a lot of people down in our district had been arrested already.

Up we went yard by yard—on our stomachs through low scrub and bushes, over the ridge itself in light, open woods, and down again in the same way. One more valley and one more ridge before we were on the Trolldalen side.

There! We jumped up again, only to be seen by a machine-gun post! There was a hail of bullets—and another wild chase downhill with new, well-rested pursuers hot on our heels. There was firing also from a summit a little farther off; where it came from none of us knew. Another hour passed—two hours—three hours; again we managed to leave our pursuers behind.

Along the east side of Trolldalen, the mountainside makes a sheer fall from a height of some three hundred feet; that would give us another chance if we could get there. We were already well along and had reached a narrow cleft which we knew led down into the valley, but which, seen from above, seemed to end abruptly in a sheer drop.

We slid down, rounded a corner, and got onto a ledge screened by low trees. Here we remained lying without moving a muscle, afraid to breathe. We could see a number of our pursuers on the edge of the cliff, furiously discussing where we had gone; at last they agreed to separate, some going north, others south, and a few remaining where they were. Fifty yards away!

We were in a spot: how long would it be before the dogs, which we had several times heard baying on our track, came up and showed which way we had gone? How long would those fellows stay up there on the cliff? If only there was some wind to make a little noise in the trees, so that every tiny sound was not heard!

We lay as still as mice, listening. Shots were continually being fired, now near, now farther off. But they were mostly scattered shots, probably meant to frighten us; now and again we heard a burst from a machine gun whose owner thought he had seen something.

Someone was moving again up above us, was beginning to run southward; evidently they had received a signal, or had suddenly thought they heard something. We waited a few minutes and continued downward, crawling one after another to the next ledge, where we lay down again, exhausted. Not only were we in bad shape physically, but our nerves were at the breaking point.

Contrary to all common sense, we lighted a cigarette, passed it around to each of us in turn. That cigarette tasted better than any I've ever smoked.

While we lay on this ledge rain began to fall; at first only single drops, but gradually increasing to a steady downpour. This was our salvation—for the time being! The trees began to drip, and the stillness of death, which previously had made our predicament so completely hopeless, was replaced by the pattering of raindrops on leaves. At the same time there came a faint breeze which increased the noise.

We went on down toward the bottom of the valley, over ground that was steep and rough and consisted of loose stones. It was a quarter-past-five; the hunt had been going on for seven hours almost without a break. We were all three soaking wet, first with perspiration and later from the rain. Now it was beginning to get cold: we had thrown away the sweaters we were carrying when the chase began and were only in our shirts, which were torn to shreds.

Which of us set the stone rolling I do not know, but

one stone started others rolling with it, causing a mini-
ature landslide. In our ears it was a fearful noise, and
we lay breathless without moving a finger.

A shot—two—three. We still lay where we were, till
we could hear one or two men coming up from the
bottom of the valley. Again we rushed downhill—along
Trolldalen northward, with one or more pursuers after
us. This time they did not seem to be in such good
training; at any rate, we managed to keep our distance. Down to the very bottom of the valley we ran;
up the river in its actual bed, sometimes in the water
and sometimes on the stones. If dogs were used, we
would still have a chance.

All three of us were now as good as done for; our
legs would not carry us any longer—they grew heavier
with every minute that passed. We had stabbing pains
in our chests, and I felt as if my heart were going to
burst.

A gigantic rock on each side of the river closed the
valley; at this point the path had been made three
feet wide to enable people to get through at all. On
each side of the gigantic rocks were sheer walls. This
would be our last chance. Hjelm and Rolf went on a
little farther and took cover, while I remained behind
one of the huge rocks.

From where we lay hidden, we saw a man come in
sight. It looked as if he too had difficulty in running;
now and then he almost came to a stop, as if too tired
to go on. He was a hundred yards away—fifty.

I fired three shots in quick succession. The German
flung himself to the ground, and a moment later, as
though shot from a cannon, he ran up the side of the

valley among some big rocks. From there he fired back three shots—but he had only a rifle, no automatic weapons. The shots went far up into the hillside, on the opposite side to where I lay. The man was not aiming at all; he must have been afraid for his life, or else he overestimated us.

Under cover of the great rock, I ran on and joined Hjelm and Rolf, who had found the place we knew about and were trying to reach: a narrow cleft in the hillside, invisible from the path up through Trolldalen, running southwest at a sharp angle toward the top of the next ridge. With great effort we reached a point about a hundred feet up and lay there behind some bushes, from which the path was in sight.

We had been there only a few minutes when the same German at whom I had fired stole past! He was not a young man and hardly a woodsman, nor was he one of the best turned-out of the mountain troops. We lay there for another quarter of an hour without stirring. All was quiet again, except for scattered shots farther east. Then came another series of shots from a machine gun, but this time farther north in Trolldalen.

What happened up on the moor after that I remember only in broad outline. We reached the top of that ridge, got past a machine-gun post without being detected, down on the other side, and lay under some bushes till it was nearly dark, while the rain poured down without a break.

During this time we had a chance to work out some kind of a plan based on several alternative courses. While Hjelm and Rolf remained where they were, I made a brief reconnaissance down to Bjor Lake, a little farther south. Here all was quiet, and it looked as if the Germans had not expected us to get so far west by that time.

I tried my luck at an out-of-the-way farm, but found only an old woman of eighty or more. As she was almost stone deaf and I did not want to ask questions at the top of my voice, I got no information from her. But I did get a mug of milk, which did wonders for my spirits.

When I regained the spot where the others lay hidden, all was still comparatively quiet. Only occasional gunshots from farther east continued with varying strength.

We made our way cautiously back to the old woman's farm. And now we decided to take a last chance. With about five hundred yards between us, we walked down the open road to our own neighborhood.

It had stopped raining, and the machine-gun posts on the moor and other high ground undoubtedly heard people going along the road. A few shots were fired, the bullets striking the water fifty yards below the road. But we went on walking openly, without checking our steps for a moment, as if we were Germans or people with perfectly clear consciences from the farms nearby.

Our impudence paid off! When the Germans got no reaction to the shots fired to scare us, they stopped after a few attempts. Little did they know that we walked with our hearts in our mouths every foot of the way.

Now the vital question was: the suspension bridge

over the river—was it guarded? If it was, we could all swim, and this would be our only choice. We came to the group of farms which lay close to where the suspension bridge crossed to Aabel. There was light behind the curtains, and as we passed someone peeped out curiously and drew back again at once.

At the bridge not a soul was to be seen. Yard by yard I went over to the other side, while Hjelm and Rolf stood waiting for a minute. If no shot came, the road was clear and they could continue up to Aabel.

Our plan, based entirely on impudence, had succeeded. Just as we had all reached the farmyard the first car passed. It was a German car—the police patrol on the Sörland Road.

It was nearly midnight, and the people at Aabel had gone to bed long before. But in a little while we were sitting with Anders and Sören Aabel at a well-laden table down in the cellar, while the two women of the family stuffed us with food. While we sat there eating, we told them what had happened. Cars were continually passing the window, since the Sörland Road ran close by.

Police cars had been about all day, the family told us; twelve persons had been arrested, including members of the Birkenes, Rugsland, and Hauge families. What had happened to the schoolmaster Daland no one knew for certain at that time; but it was rumored that he had been in bed when the Germans came, and his wife had told them that he was very ill and had been in bed for the last few days. So they let him alone. This rumor proved later to be correct.

In short, it was now only a question of time before

the Aabel family had visitors; we three, therefore, as a precaution, agreed to Anders' proposal that we should go for a little walk up to the moor toward Röynaas, on the opposite side of the valley, where the great hunt was still going on.

For two days we lay buried in the hay in the outside loft of the Aabel farm; Anders kept us informed of the latest developments in the neighborhood and supplied us with food. Our clothes were in a sorry state after the chase, so when we decided to make a trip into town we had to borrow clothes from Anders.

But how should we get to the town, with the road patrolled and guards and police driving up and down at all hours of the day?

Spaced at half-hour intervals, we sauntered down the road from Aabel to Drangsholdt, about a twenty-minute walk. Rolf started earliest that morning, for he planned to take a bus, which went into town by a different route.

Hjelm was to go last, as he was to take the same bus I took, but from a stopping point farther down. There was a good deal of police-car traffic on the roads as each of us went to his own place in the early-morning hours. But who would guess that the persons for whom hundreds had been searching for three days and nights would be following the same road the police used most—especially when the last track led northward through Trolldalen and the men had probably tried to get to the Sörland train somewhere in the vicinity of Ogge Lake? It was there that the patrols were most heavily concentrated.

While I sat waiting for my bus, and one police car

after another passed, a solitary workman came down the road. It was Hjelm. He looked in no way different from all the other workmen who started out at that time of morning. Hjelm passed me without moving a muscle, and on to the next bus stop.

It was almost comic later, when we were sitting in the same bus—Hjelm and two senior German officers who had got in at Boen, and another workman who looked remarkably like Rolf. Something unforeseen must have occurred, but we did not find out until later what had prevented him from taking the other bus.

Rolf got off seven miles outside Kristiansand; Hjelm got off four-and-a-half miles outside, and I went right on in. At the beginning of Kongsgaard Allé; just before one entered the town, there was a control, but it was a superficial one. Everything went astonishingly well, and we all met the same evening at our contact's house in Oesterveien.

The problem now was how to get away from Kristiansand. Would the railway be watched? Would the Kristiansand-Oslo boat be watched? All communications from Kristiansand would probably be controlled for the time being; but to what extent? Telephone communication between Arendal, Grimstad, Lillesand, Kristiansand, and Mandal had already been stopped.

It was decided to send Rolf by train to Oslo next morning, as he was too well-known to people in the countryside and to those who had already been arrested. Despite the risk of a police visit to the house at any hour, the family offered to shelter us for the night.

Arne's father, a guard on the line from Kristiansand

to Oslo, was now, as usual, willing to take Rolf with him on the train. He was one of the many people in the service of the Norwegian State Railways who did indescribably brilliant work in the war. He was over sixty-five, but as vigorous as a man half his age and always willing to take over a share of the duties which were specially imposed on the youth of Norway. Because of his help Rolf's journey went well, despite snoopers and police at a number of stations.

Later in the week we resumed contact with London from Ovrebö, and communicated the unfortunate result of the parachute drop. At the same time we sent off important reports and information in reply to a series of questions we had received from London just before the drop. These questions related to the net defenses of the port of Kristiansand and covered the following points:

Were the nets antitorpedo, antisubmarine, or antisurface vessel?

What was the distance between buoys?

How long was the net in the different sections and what was the position of moorings?

How were the nets moored and what kind of yielding system was used?

What influence had ice or other objects had on the net?

How thick was the wire between the buoys, and how many strands were used?

What was the depth of the net? The size of meshes? The thickness and number of strands in the mesh wire? Was it anchored to the bottom; if so, by what means?

Was the net connected with acoustic or magnetic mines outside it?

At first we scratched our heads in bewilderment on receiving this string of questions. The whole thing seemed hopeless, but in a little while a number of lucky circumstances made it possible for us to answer them all. By using our three principal contacts, who in turn used every source they had, we got the answers one after another.

The amusing part about it was the way in which it became possible to obtain the answers. A Swedish ship which was to enter Kristiansand for examination "unluckily missed the opening in the net when entering after dark." At a good clip she went straight into the net, taking a whole section of it with her into the quayside.

The net had to be sent to the naval yard at Marvika for repairs—and at Marvika there were two men, one of whom was a contact of Arne and the other of Johan, the customs official. Johan's contact helped repair the net; at the same time he did an excellent job for us. Between them, our contacts did all the work, and we had only to put the results together.

Months later I found out what lay behind the questions. The British were after the *Tirpitz*, the 41,000-ton battleship which it had taken the Germans five years to build at a cost of fifty million dollars.

At the time, the ship had no connection with the port of Kristiansand; but information collected from various sources indicated that nets like those used at Kristiansand and Stavanger were also in use at Altafjord to protect the *Tirpitz*. The difference here was only that the nets were double and in places were connected with mines. In the Altafjord it was practically impossible to get any detailed information about the nets, and the only chance was to get this from Kristiansand and Stavanger.

It was not until 1944 that the British finally got the *Tirpitz*. On November 12, twenty-nine Lancaster bombers suddenly emerged from the arctic mists off Tromsö and sank the pride of the German navy.

11 Back to Kristiansand

WE DIDN'T HAVE MUCH TIME to get ready for the invasion. June, I had gathered, was to be the crucial month. The head office had been established in Oslo; all the parcels sent from Darbu had arrived and been distributed; a regular messenger service to and from Kristiansand had been arranged through our earlier contacts on this route, as well as a messenger service to and from Sweden and a number of sources of information in the area around Oslo.

On May 28, I went to Kristiansand myself. All journeys over this route were to be made by night train, because up to now most examinations had been made on the day trains. Only when something out of the ordinary had happened were controls put on the night train, too. I made the trip down without any trouble. I got off next morning at a wayside station, and went on by train an hour later. All was quiet at Mosby, my destination, about seven miles from Kristiansand.

I then cycled up to the country around Ovrebö, where the proposed main station was to be established. I had a pleasant reunion with Gunnar Upsahl, our main contact in those parts in earlier days, and there were no difficulties about starting a new station.

The old hut was still at our disposal, and father and son had made great improvements since we had last occupied it.

On the afternoon of May 29 I opened contact with England on the electrical circuit from the house itself. The station would start a full service the next day.

Jan and Lars joined me a few days later; they too had an untroubled journey down, although for Lars this trip to Kristiansand involved a certain amount of special danger. Not too long ago, he had had to flee for his life from that particular area; now, if he met anyone he knew on the train, he might as well turn around and go right back, otherwise he might be followed, endangering all of us. But although he saw a few acquaintances on the journey, he actually met no one.

Weather reports were then among the most important information we could send to London. Our orders ran, "if possible from June 1 at latest." Most of the material which we had originally planned to use in Southern Norway had arrived at Mosby and Kristiansand in good condition. But the all-important radio equipment we had brought down with us in parcels.

Gunnar now walked down to the railway station, collected the various packages which had come, and took them up to Ovrebö openly by bus. Most of the things from Oslo were picked up in the same way on later occasions. If there was a control, we heard about it in good time, as Gunnar himself sometimes drove the regular bus and knew the different drivers.

Now and then something unexpected happened here as elsewhere; but Gunnar was always the man to get our things through. When I think about the different ways in which we moved dangerous things from one place to another, I am amazed that it always ended well.

There were controls almost everywhere, and our stuff usually lay unconcealed. As a rule, in fact, the Germans could move our "treasure chest" and stand on it—even sit and rest on it after a tiring search, yet whole radio sets, arms and ammunition, code books, and deciphered reports went through their hands daily.

We had several busy days digging hiding places around the hut; the order was that anything which could possibly betray the nature of our work was to be removed Only the "holy of holies," the little bag containing the code books, weather-report tables, message books, and all the other things that had to be used daily to draft each separate message, had to be in the hut most of the day.

At night, when we had finished drafting the day's messages, this little bag, too, was hidden outside in a place used only for this purpose. Occasionally we contacted London during the night; but the "holy of holies" was always hidden immediately afterward.

Weather reports were sent every morning at 8:00 A.M. Greenwich Mean Time. Up at the observation post we noted the height and types of clouds, the force and direction of the wind, visibility, "dry" and "wet" temperature, relative humidity; we gave a general review of the weather in the last twelve hours, made barometric readings, and reported any other conditions which might interest the compiler of a weather forecast across the sea.

To the best of my knowledge, we were the only

station in Norway which gave detailed weather reports, and these were of great importance for all operations from England over Europe as a whole.

These weather reports increased the chance that the Germans might locate the radio station by direction-finding. It was impossible for us to vary the times of our meteorological messages much, as the observations had to be taken at a fixed time every day, and the reports had to be at the Air Ministry within an hour and a half so they could be included in the morning weather charts which were sent out to all operational bases under Allied Command.

Furthermore, every single meteorological message went on the same frequency and with the same call sign every day. But the messages went only in numbers; the frequency was the best we had; and we were able to maintain a high rate of speed.

In these conditions, even if the German radio stations did their best to locate the signals by direction-finding, and after a short period of activity observed the meteorological message every morning, there was little chance of their finding us. Numbers are much more difficult to trace down than letters, as the message goes in a rapid staccato.

If big things were brewing, we usually received a "crack signal" after the morning weather report in the shape of a five-figure number. "Big things" were, for example, large-scale bombings of Berlin or other important targets. The five-figure number meant that we were to send additional weather reports at two fixed times later in the same day; if there were two separate five-figure groups, we were to send weather reports every other hour throughout the twenty-four hours, until new instructions were received.

Naturally, we listened eagerly to the next day's news report to learn where the operation had taken place and what result had been achieved—and in a modest way we liked to credit ourselves with a small share in the result.

The first week of June many of these "crack signals" came. On June 5 reports were sent every other hour. June 6: INVASION!

What joyous news that was! I shall not forget the faces of people in Kristiansand when they heard the news, long before the Germans had pulled themselves together and realized what was happening. People stood in small groups eagerly discussing the invasion; the Germans who suddenly found themselves very busy seemed just shabby little creatures scurrying along. But this impression did not last long; as the days passed and the Allied invasion gained more ground, the "Master Race" became more and more hysterical and their actions more and more aggressive.

Our own work was to become more strenuous than ever. At this time there was a big upheaval among our connections in Kristiansand itself. Special circumstances brought about a complete change of sources and contacts in the sector. The change involved a complete recasting of our method of work, which required above all a keen, reliable nucleus of people with only one aim—to work for the cause without regard to personal interests.

Our connections in Kristiansand during 1943 had made a splendid contribution to the cause. Worthy of particular commendation were the railway guard in Oesterveien, his son, and the rest of his family. The guard's unfailing helpfulness on the Oslo-Kristiansand route was invaluable to us. He was now transferred to the Kristiansand-Stavanger line, but before he left his old position he found first-class people to take over, and they gave us wholehearted co-operation and considerable help all through 1944.

The contacts we already had in the country districts —in Tveit, Birkenes, and Oddernes—were still used whenever possible. But inevitably individual members of the organization became a little too well-known to the people of these parts. In the town, on the other hand, there was a complete change of personnel.

To deal with the shipping in the port of Kristiansand was still our most important task. But this was now to be attacked in quite a different way, in accordance with a plan gradually developed in collaboration with the British Command. Individuals were to play an important part in this plan, so secret but exhaustive inquiries were made about all the candidates suggested.

Here is how the plan would work: Sven Nordahl-Hansen was employed by the Norwegian Harbor Police and was on duty from eight o'clock every night until eight in the morning in that part of the Kristiansand quay system which most interested us. His work brought Sven into regular contact with warrant and petty officers and seamen of the German Navy who were under the command of the harbor captain.

Through the office of the harbor captain went all information about every ship arriving at or sailing from Kristiansand, and every convoy: names, tonnage, cargo, armament, destination, escorts of convoys and their armament, the convoy's most secret call signs at different times of day and night, and a lot of other details which were of the greatest interest to us.

The question now was this: Among his German connections, could Sven find one or two who were willing to start work within the area of the German harbor captain?

When the plan was first proposed the whole thing seemed too risky, and we agreed to wait and see how things developed. Since Sven himself would run the greatest risk, it was finally left to him to decide whether the plan was feasible. There were two men in particular in the harbor, German warrant officers, who seemed to have different political views and higher moral standards than most of the Germans. As much attention as possible was therefore given to these two, but without the others' suspecting the developing "friendship."

It was the men themselves who made the first advance; their plan was not to carry out espionage, but to desert, steal the German Harbor Police's speedboat which lay moored every night where they could get at it, load it with food and equipment stolen from the naval depot close by—and set a course at full speed for England!

Would Sven, as a man who knew the local terrain, accompany them along the coast? Despite the so-called friendship between the two parties, there was marked suspicion on both sides, and at first Sven seemed skeptical about the plan.

The possibilities were discussed next day in the attic of Sven's home. It was obviously a choice of risks. If the two Germans were told that Sven would have nothing to do with the plan, or that he would report them if they put it into action—what then? Would not Sven be in danger of getting a bullet in his back some dark night?

It would be easy for two Germans to fake a story about sabotage or something of the kind. There was even a chance that the whole thing was an *agent provocateur* plot. If the Germans were to accept Sven's proposal that they remain in their positions and start co-operation with an "illegal organization," what assurance had we that they would not give the whole thing away to the Gestapo? Also, what guarantee had we that the information they gave was correct? How could a security system be established in the event they accepted the plan?

If, on the other hand, such co-operation were successful, it might be more important to the Allied cause than anything we had yet accomplished.

The plan was laid before both Germans at once, because we recognized another factor which made for safety. If there was only one man, he could easily change his mind after a time and withdraw; if there were two, this would be considerably more difficult. A little to our surprise, they accepted, and apparently with great enthusiasm, although it had been made clear to them that there could be no monetary reward. Our principle was work for a cause on idealistic grounds; if their efforts were inspired by a desire for personal gain, the results would undoubtedly be less satisfactory. The guarantee we could offer, in case anything went wrong, was a "free" journey to Sweden or straight to England.

The Germans received their instructions, through Sven, on thin paper in newspapers, cigarettes, bread, and similar ordinary articles of exchange. They were told what interested us most, how the reports should be compiled, and how often the regular harbor reports should be given. Highly important to us was the fact that these two men had practically unlimited access to all secrets in the harbor captain's offices.

For a month the work went full-steam ahead. In addition to the station in Ovrebö, we had for the second time an auxiliary station a mile or two outside the town. The information supplied us by our German friends was first-class. Here is how we made sure of that: we asked questions to which we already had the right answers, and were thus able to check the accuracy of their work and gradually establish their value to us.

After only a month, they had the sinking of two German ships to their credit, and that settled matters. From then on they were entirely in our hands; if they tried trickery of any kind, it would be a simple matter for us to put a nice collection of cigarette papers, on which their reports were written, in an envelope, and send it anonymously to Gestapo headquarters in Kristiansand.

Sven above all was secure, at least so long as the two Germans were at large, and they themselves were politely and cautiously made aware of the position. Any carelessness on their part would react first of all on themselves.

I have said that we set up an auxiliary station south-

west of Kristiansand for the *second* time. The first
occasion, some time before, deserves brief mention.
The main station in Ovrebö was at times too far from
town for complete efficiency. When the port was very
busy and large convoys were leaving, the reports about
them reached the station too late unless we had advance information.

Several locations were considered for an auxiliary
station, which must be only a mile or two from town.
We had brought with us from England a good 1,500
feet of insulated double-strand rubber cable, intend-
ing to use it for an auxiliary station on the "Upturned
Boat," where we had a station the year before. The
electric circuit along the Södal Road, where the current was 210 volts A.C., would be tapped with a free
wire into a fixed watertight plug box, well hidden
under the root of a tree or a large stone.

From here the rubber cable, buried and screened,
would run up the hillside to a ledge where I had
figured on having a charging station for the batteries.
This ledge, about sixty feet from the top, was well-
covered by trees and bushes, and difficult to see either
from above or from below. The station itself I had
thought of placing where it was in 1943. From the
ledge we had a fine view of the entire harbor, over
the whole approach from both west and east, and in
clear weather for many miles west toward Mandal.

After a brief reconnaissance, however, we were
forced to reject this plan. The Germans had set up
their big radio station about three-quarters of a mile
away, and a regular guard was mounted there; fifty
yards below the top there was a German area, which

was patrolled at regular intervals; at the farm below
the cliff, where the path went up, a large contingent
of German soldiers and horses were quartered; in
short, we couldn't have chosen a less suitable location
for our station.

The terrain on every side of the town was combed
without success. You can't set up a radio station just
anywhere and start tapping. Hundreds of problems
are involved, both technical and practical. Moreover,
it seemed that whenever we found a place we liked,
the Germans had already discovered it and installed
something or other there or in the immediate neighborhood.

So it happened that the country west of Augland
Bay was the only practicable ground left, in spite of
its being completely surrounded by the strongest
military installations in Kristiansand. In the first place
there were the Mövig fortifications a short way outside town, and we were compelled to use the road
going right past them. Then there were great military
constructions to the south, a camp with gigantic pill-
boxes along the road south toward the lake, and large
ammunition dumps to the north. All these lay in a
circle within a two-mile radius of the Auxiliary station.

Small wonder, then, that every word uttered while
we were there had to be whispered; rubber shoes had
to be used, no matter how fine the weather; in short,
it was a game of hide-and-seek twenty-four hours a
day. Yet it was worth all the risks, despite our dis-
agreeable neighbors, because the site had wonderful
possibilities. We had one great, indispensable advantage: the ground around the station was very rough,

and people frequenting those parts were more or less confined to the regular paths.

We set up our first camp on the southern side of Barlindal Moor itself. The main tent was well-covered with fresh conifer boughs reinforced with thick deciduous foliage. The camouflaged kitchen tent, a few yards away, was close to a rock face and similarly covered; and the radio tent about ten yards from the main tent was hidden in a small depression in the ground.

We were able to run this first auxiliary station for four weeks more or less in peace and with excellent results. We received advance reports, as much as twenty-four hours beforehand, of every convoy that left Kristiansand Harbor. From the top of Barlindal Moor, in a patch of scrub, we had a first-class view over the whole harbor and exit. Thus, we could note the sailing and arrival of every ship, compare these with the advance reports from our two German collaborators, and give London exact information.

It could not have been very pleasant being harbor captain at that time; such a distressing number of ships never reached their destinations.

There was every chance of our being located by direction-finding. The Nazis had a radio station not far away, and in addition to this the Germans had every opportunity of taking cross-bearings from the various fortifications in the neighborhood, and with direction-finding cars from all the roads around the area. Certainly we had Barlindal Moor behind us with its southwesterly rock face, which gave considerable protection and served as a reflector for the station.

But our only real security consisted in reports from a contact within the police, who was attached to the police radio section.

He was able to tell us now and then how far the Germans had got in locating the station which they had long known to exist somewhere in the immediate neighborhood of Kristiansand. But of course there was the constant danger that, just once, he might not get all the information we needed for our protection.

12   Even the Birds Give Warning

While we were running our first auxiliary station up in the Barlindal district, we were benefited by a rather strange phenomenon. From time to time, as we crept about to avoid being detected, sat eating outside the main tent, or were busy with contact, coding, or other work, we would suddenly stop and listen intently. One of the camp's two "watchdogs" was warning us; something was coming up the valley on one side or down the steep gully on the other.

These "watchdogs" happened to be two pairs of birds—blackbirds and stonechats, respectively. The blackbirds were always in the narrow cleft that led up from the valley toward the camp, the stonechats in the gully down from the moor itself. If anything disturbed either of these two pairs of birds they uttered cries of a definite kind which, after a short time, we learned to recognize. The cause of the excitement might be a sheep, a hunting hawk, a fox, or some other wild creature.

But it could also be a two-legged intruder. These often disturbed us; but without exception the visitors were always "announced" beforehand by one pair of birds or the other, so that we could take security measures. Yet the visitors always went past our door without seeing us, sometimes only a yard away from the main tent where we sat and could follow them with a machine gun or revolver.

By degrees an amusing game developed between the German Police Radio Section and our station, sometimes very amusing indeed for us. I learned from our source within their ranks that the Germans suspected the district in which we were operating, and the direction-finding cars began more concentrated surveillance of the roads around.

Lars was now sent up to Ovrebö with the crystals or frequencies we had been working on for a long time. Using the same call signs and at the same time of day, he sent off the message from the main station, many miles from the district where the Germans were sure they would find us. Suddenly, only a day or two before they planned to go through the district with a fine-tooth comb, the signals came in from an entirely different direction and became much weaker. So they were back where they had started, and all they could do was go right back to the beginning again.

Lars continued to send from Ovrebö for a week; at the same time, we at the auxiliary station had begun to work on different wave lengths, at different times, and with new call signs. We also reduced our sending to an absolute minimum.

Unfortunately, it was not only the Germans who worried us. I was obliged to cycle into Kristiansand about every other day to work on plans and discuss their execution with our various connections. If the station got into contact with London while I was in town, Lars and Jan took over, and very competently. But I was involved in a lot of gadding-about along the road to town, coming back the same day or the next.

I'm sure the people at the local shop had already begun to wonder where we were, having guessed from the things we bought that there were several of us. But there were many strangers working for the Germans at Mövig; they probably thought we belonged to the same crowd. Nevertheless, we tried hard to reach the moor at different points, so that the people who lived closest to us there would not continually notice our movements.

Things went well, too, for a fairly long time—about a month the first time. Regular messengers came out from town with the latest news and food; the food situation was now considerably better. Three different "barter centers" were in full swing; there tobacco could be traded for butter, cheese, or other foodstuffs. Some of this was sent in a special manner down to Kristiansand, collected regularly by the same people, and brought out to us; some was sent from stations upcountry direct into Oslo for distribution among the contacts there.

At the station we were unfortunately restricted to a monotonous diet, since lighting a fire was forbidden. We used a primus stove, and its hissing in the kitchen tent, which was well covered up, could not be heard more than a few yards away. Only on very still evenings did we have to stop using it. Our menu, therefore, was simple: bread and butter with something on it, oat gruel "floating" in butter—the same thing three times a day, with tea or coffee. It became monotonous at times, but it was adequate, especially since we hardly had time to eat anyway.

The station was run entirely on batteries. A regular contact down in Augland had undertaken this part of the work. The transformer was built into a small box on the wall of a garage, and the batteries were placed for charging overnight and hidden next morning.

It was Jan's job, at appointed times on certain days of the week, to carry the used batteries on a forty-five-minute walk to a prearranged "post office" in the woods. When he arrived there, he had only to exchange them for a set of fully charged batteries. The used batteries were collected later the same evening and placed for charging.

It was now July 26, and a steadily increasing stream of summer tourists past the station had disturbed our idyll for a week or more. We had had two visits from a Storch plane, and the last time we were convinced that it definitely suspected our position. For more than an hour it circled around the top of Barlindal, swept down low over the station, and came back the same way.

It was about nine in the morning. Jan was sitting in the main tent darning socks; Lars was down in the valley getting water, and I was over in the radio tent coding a report of one of the largest convoys we had had that summer. All in all, it was a really peaceful idyll. Then a branch cracked up in the gully, and a small stone slithered down into the scree.

The stonechat began to chatter, followed by the

blackbird in the cleft running down into the valley. I jumped up, stowed code books and everything connected with them away in the bag, and fastened the bag around my waist. It could not be Lars, as the stonechat up in the gully had sounded the alarm first, so the noise had come from there. It must be visitors.

A sudden thought occurred to me where I sat—the aerial! It had just been hung up, as we were scheduled to contact London in a quarter of an hour. Well, it was too late to start fooling with that—people had walked right under it before without seeing it. I crept over to the main tent, warned Jan, caught up a Sten gun, and stood half outside, covered by the camouflage over the tent.

Whoever was coming was obviously a practiced woodsman; we could hardly hear him. There was a movement in the bushes fifteen yards away from the tent; that meant the man was following the sheep track which passed three yards away. Then we saw him as he stopped and looked all around as if searching for something. He had an axe under his arm. At any rate we could see he was not a German—evidently he was the owner of the timber or one of his workmen.

Now he began to fell some small trees ten or twelve yards away from the main tent. I remained standing where I was, bent forward, and tried to keep Jan posted on what was happening. The man was beginning to make a sheep fence on the side where the aerial was fastened!

Row after row was felled, and the man moved slowly but surely toward the tree to which the aerial was fastened. Each time, before he felled a tree, he

looked up to judge whether it was suitable. There!
He was standing upright with the axe half-raised—
he had seen the aerial! I cursed to myself, and Jan
grasped what had happened from my expression.

"Give me a pencil and a notebook!" I whispered to
him.

"But what the devil is this?" The fellow stood talking to himself for a minute or two as he looked up
and along the aerial over toward the little hillock which
concealed the radio tent. He still did not see a thing
in the direction of the main tent, two yards away from
where I stood. His eyes moved this way and that, and
curiosity was written all over his face.

Then I rose. The man literally jumped with fright.
My right hand was in my pocket around my revolver.
There was no need to show our colors too much, if
it could be avoided.

"Stop, if you value your life!" I said threateningly.
Jan remained under cover with a Sten gun in his hands;
there was no sense in making it possible for the woodsman to describe more than one of us. "What are you
doing up here?" I asked.

"I own the timber!" he replied meekly.

I asked the man to show his papers; as a precaution-
ary measure I checked the various data like an ordinary
German control, and took notes. Jan, meanwhile, was
finding it hard to keep from laughing. I told the man
we were students in hiding, with a radio to help pass
the time while we waited for the invasion. I told him
that if he valued his own life he would forget what
he had seen, and keep away from the woods so long
as conditions were so unsettled.

But the fellow did not seem to have any great sympathy for students in hiding; he seemed to have his own ideas about us, although he didn't express them. But he was plainly nervous. At last I asked him to clear out in a fairly polite manner, and he disappeared in a flash toward the valley, from which we were awaiting Lars. But Lars had overheard the conversation in broken sentences, and when the man came rushing downhill he hid behind some bushes to let him pass.

The whole thing was strange and disturbing—the man's behavior and appearance, and his obvious nervousness. This became clear when, instead of continuing up the valley, as he had said he meant to do, he dashed down toward Stor Lake and took the shortest route to Augland. I followed hard on his heels right down to the next lake; now he was running for his life. But he had a boat, and in it he rowed across at top speed while I had to run all the way around the lake. Then, instead of taking the road down to Augland, he went over the moor, ruining my plan to cut him off lower down.

The whole camp was dismantled in fifteen minutes. All the radio equipment was hidden in a place prepared long before, farther down the valley. Lars went one way, Jan another, and I a third, each of us with full sacks. Not a thing was left but the remains of the camouflage we had used.

Jan and Lars did not arrive at the main station in Ovrebö till late the same evening; I took the road into Kristiansand and up to Eidet on the other side of town, after making inquiries to find out who our uninvited guest really was. Our suspicions were justified; this timber owner was the most rabid Nazi in the area.

I spent that night with the Mathisen family, whom we had met the year before when we were working up in Tveit and Birkenes. From the very first day there was never even the hint of a question as to who we were, where we came from, or what kind of work we were doing. The door was always open to us.

This place had got us out of many a difficult situation. Once I came riding along with a radio transmitter in my bicycle bag, and didn't stop for a control. It consisted of two motorcycles with three German police soldiers on each. I cycled into the Mathisens' yard, knocked, and asked if I could leave my bicycle bag while I was down at the hut which had been placed at our disposal for use when we needed it.

Yes, certainly, I could leave it either in the house or under the steps. I chose the latter, laid an old tarpaulin over the bag, and went down toward the hut just as the motorcycles swung into the yard. The Germans started to follow me, so instead of going down to the hut I went for a stroll in the neighborhood with three Germans fifteen yards behind me all the time.

None of them approached me; they probably only wanted to see what I was like and whether I was doing anything in particular. They evidently thought I had not heard them, but when I turned suddenly, they were standing and chatting as if they were not at all interested in me. Instead of giving them a wide berth, I went up to them, greeted them politely, and asked if they could sell me a cigarette. Yes, they could; one of them even gave me a light. It's hard to say which of us was more surprised at this mutual courtesy.

I took my bicycle and rode into town, leaving the radio transmitter where I had hidden it; but the woman of the house took the bag into the kitchen for the night as a precaution against its disappearance.

It was as a student for a forestry degree or wood-cutter that I now took a first-floor room with the Mathisens, and many were the tall stories told by forestry pupil 'Oeyvind Fredriksen" during the many pleasant hours spent with the family. Whether the Mathisens were deceived was quite another matter; but despite warnings from several quarters against giving lodging to "that strange man who is obviously up to something shady," I was never asked a question of a personal nature, nor was the door ever shut against me.

The day after our unwelcome caller had dropped in on our camp, I walked back to Barlindal Moor to find out if anything had happened in the meantime. This was of the greatest importance because the Nazi might by now have given a very exact description of me, and in that case it might be a good idea to alter my appearance a little.

It was raining hard, and not a soul was to be seen, either on the way or up at the camp. The rain had washed out every footmark, so possibly our veiled threats about what had happened to other informers had had some effect after all.

With the radio equipment in my sack, I made a detour down to Augland and looked in on our contact there. Yes, there had been two cars with German police out there the same morning, and they had made inquiries in the houses along the edge of the wood. He could not say what the reason was, but it was likely that the Nazi had been talking.

Well, the Germans knew. I took my bicycle and rode up to Ovrebö, but not one of the Germans I met on the road seemed to take the slightest interest either in me or in my sizable package. Jan and Lars had gone by the same road, and they had had no trouble either.

Up in Ovrebö our work was continued at full speed. We were forced to return to the messenger system, but it was now so efficiently developed that all advance reports of convoys and movements in the port reached us swiftly. The actual sailing of the convoys was telephoned up to the village shop, whose owner, Ilebaek, and his family did excellent work throughout the summer and autumn of 1944. The so-called "vegetable code" was used.

The radio station itself was now located about two hundred yards from Upsahl farm in a small hut, partly buried in the ground and covered by a large boulder. The current was tapped by a rather ingenious installation down in the barn, connected with a fixed rubber cable which was buried in the ground and ran to a junction box under the root of a tree about twenty yards from the radio hut. At contact times we had to run an extra cable to the apparatus which, when we were not using it, lay hidden in a watertight container buried a short way below the wood.

The amusing thing about this main station was that from where the man on duty sat during contact he could follow all traffic on the road and at the same time keep an eye on a large German camp a couple of hundred yards above Upsahl farm. An officer from the camp had been to Upsahl and asked if he could buy milk. That was why we preferred not to establish contact from the farm itself, though we were sometimes compelled to do so when time was short; but it would be unfortunate if the German officer's visit were repeated.

A little after six every evening was also a very unfavorable time. We could sit on the rock above the farm and observe person after person coming with a milk pail, as we used to do to conceal our activity from too interested people. One man after another came loafing along, went through the door into the house, but did not come out again.

At twenty-five minutes past six, one of the two sons of the house came out, sauntered over to the barn, and returned in a minute or two carrying a large box. If you then paid a visit to a small room upstairs, you were sure to find it crowded—the whole family and a few near neighbors would be sitting, absorbed, about the radio listening to the London news while a member of the family kept watch at the window which overlooked the road and the German camp.

A continued series of questions streamed into our station from the Allied Supreme Command, questions which taxed our imaginations as we tried to determine their purpose. They were all connected with the invasion, which was now in full swing, and all touched upon the possibility of which we were all thinking in those days—would there be an Allied invasion of Norway?

One message read as follows:

Is there a divisional staff in Arendal? Give number, HQ, and name of CO.

Is there a Grenadier regiment's HQ in Kristiansand South, and/or in Lyngdal? Give number, location of HQ, and name of CO.

Are the Army troops in Mandal subordinated to Lyngdal or Kristiansand?

Is there an Army Coastal Artillery regiment's HQ in Kristiansand? Give location and name of CO.

Command of coast defenses:

1. Are coast defenses in the Naval Commandant's area divided into operational groups, with, for example, one in Kristiansand, one in Arendal, etc.?

2. Are any of the Army Coastal Artillery troops subordinated to the Naval Commandant for operational purposes?

3. Are any of the Army Coastal Artillery troops under command of O.C. Battle Group?

4. Give liaison center of coast defense.

Try to get a list of all vessels under the orders of the Naval Commandant.

Get the number of the regimental staff at Borgestad, near Porsgrunn, and name of CO.

Give location of battalion HQ's in division. Are there battalion HQ's in Kristiansand, Evjemoen, Birkeland, and Arendal?

How are the division field artillery, antitank artillery, and reconnaissance battalion disposed?

This was only one series of questions, and I include

it to illustrate the kind of extra work that was required
of us, in addition to the ordinary information we sent
about shipping movements in the districts, information which undoubtedly gave the most visible results.
Thanks to our tireless associates and our two German
friends, every question in the above message was
answered in a comparatively short time.

For a few weeks we were to be able to take it easy
up in Ovrebö, at least by comparison with the life we
were compelled to lead on Barlindal Moor. It was
something to be able to talk out loud and not have to
go about whispering to one another all day; not to
sleep uneasily every night, revolver always in hand;
not to have to wake Lars every time he began to
snore, or shake Jan whenever he talked in his sleep
or dreamed that he was fighting twenty-five Germans
singlehanded!

At the main station we were able to establish a very
dependable warning system in case of suspicious traffic
on the road. People up there had begun to grow accustomed to the three townsmen who lived in the hut
up by Stoess Lake. An avowed Nazi lived nearby,
they pointed out, so despite the rumors they could
not be very dangerous. People from the district were
constantly up there bathing, and we joined them for
a little relaxation whenever we could.

Meanwhile, the road between Kristiansand and
Ovrebö was becoming more dangerous to travel. As
the invasion of France steadily progressed, the Germans seemed to become more and more savage; there
was always a control on the road, especially at the
outskirts of the town.

We particularly disliked the main road past Mosby, and therefore used the Södal Road on the other side of the river. The Germans had discovered that it was safer for them to live outside the town, and had evacuated all the larger camps and were quartering their men and equipment outside, in the various farms up the valley. As a result, practically all the farms up in the Södal countryside were occupied. But as far as we were concerned, this turned out to be an advantage.

The Germans were less anxious about illegal traffic along these roads, and consequently relaxed their controls.

13   An Inch or Two
from the Archives

On Sunday, September 17, I really had a close call. In the last few months, the controls had been growing steadily more severe. The controls in themselves were usually not too dangerous, so long as one didn't have a sack full of things which could not bear inspection. But even if everything was in order in that respect, and even if one had no packages at all, it still was not uncommon for someone to be detained for "closer examination."

For this reason we chose Sunday as the best day for moving supplies and equipment from one place to another. Most of the people out for walks on Sunday carried parcels of some sort; one more wouldn't make any difference.

We had to bring a few spare parts for the American transmitter we were now using from a little storage dump we had up at Eidet. In addition, there were some clothes and tobacco that I wanted to get up to Ovrebö.

On the way into town there was the usual control at Mosby, but as a rule this was easy to get past. Nor should the control down the Södal Road cause any difficulties, judging by previous experience. I was now fairly well acquainted with the men who were usually on duty there, and as a rule they waved me on without stopping, whether I had a package or not. They had had to listen too often to the long list of dates, names, and German local commands I had worked for in the last year.

Up at the crossroads, where the Sörland Road comes into Kongsgaard Allé, there was no sign of a control.

As usual I spent the greater part of the day up at Eidet, bathed with some of the young people from the country around, and heard the latest crop of rumors, facts, and fancies. The Mathisen family were able to tell me about the extent and kind of traffic along the Sörland Road, and even give me accurate information on the number of vehicles in military convoys; all, naturally, in the course of a general conversation during which neither of the parties displayed any open interest.

My troubles started on the way home. I took the road toward town along with the stream of other cyclists who had been out after black-market food up in the valley. I had a rucksack that was not conspicuously large; it was, in fact, like all the others. I rode at fair speed down the slope toward the crossroads where the Kongsgaard Allé began.

Then I went cold for a moment, for I suddenly saw a control! Not an ordinary control, but at least twelve or fifteen men in full marching order; they wore helmets and carried machine guns.

For a moment I thought of putting on my brakes,

turning off the road, and attempting to escape, but there was a barbed-wire fence and a long field without a scrap of cover. It was too late anyhow—I was now only fifteen or twenty yards away from them. I would try to ride through without slowing down—pretend not to hear—no, there were German police soldiers a good way farther down.

"Halt! Halt! Pass control! Halt, there!" A German officer brandishing a machine gun nearly hurled me off my bicycle as I braked as hard as I could, skidded past, and did not stop till I ran into a tree ten yards lower down, after nearly knocking another soldier off his legs. The officer raged—the soldier abused me roundly—a hundred times I begged for *"Verzeihung"* —forgiveness.

Was I trying to dodge the control? Didn't I understand German? Didn't I understand what halt meant? I pleaded bad brakes—I hadn't noticed the control till I was right into it—again a hundred times *"Verzeihung."*

My flow of speech was suddenly checked; three Norwegians with bicycles and large packages were standing by the roadside with their hands up; one man, also with a large package and a bicycle, was standing in the middle of the road, while two Germans were spreading out the contents of his sack. Another German was about to search him. There was certainly little chance for me at this time—nor later, if I was arrested now.

The officer stood for a moment looking at the men who were being searched; then he turned to me. "Passport!" he demanded. There was no "please" this time.

Name, age, residence, profession, where I had been, where I was going—the usual catechism. Yes, all of that was certainly in order, but, "Hands up," he suddenly ordered, and prepared to search me!

I grew cold—the revolver! It was in the shoulder holster that was now stretched around my waist, so that the weapon itself lay in the top of my crotch. Pockets—under my arms—around my belt and alongside the outside of my thighs—off with my rubber boots, and—up the inside of my trouser-leg—around the lower edge of my drawers.

At that moment another man with a full rucksack bore down on us, and he also seemed to have difficulty in stopping. The officer rose suddenly when only a few inches from the critical point, and cursed at the new arrival.

I remained standing with my hands up, while the German almost exploded with rage. Then he turned to me again, and I could see that he had forgotten for the moment how far he had gone. Yes—his thoughts were written plainly in the wrinkles on his forehead. It looked as if he had finished!

Then the rucksack! A cold sweat once more began to run down my back. It was inevitable! The man in charge of the control stood looking at the Germans who had now set to work examining the next man's luggage. Yes, it looked as if they had enough to do.

I was still standing with my hands up, trying to seem uninterested despite my nervousness. The German took three long steps, grasped the bicycle from behind, and lifted it up. Weight in proportion to size was evidently what interested him. He dropped the back part on to the road from eighteen inches above the ground, listening as he did so. No, there were no weapons there at any rate.

Next he pressed the sack and its pockets, and asked: "What have you got here?"

"Apples, working clothes," and then came the usual story about my being a forestry pupil.

The officer looked at the others again; could they take the next man? No, they were only half finished—then he came back to me again, looked me straight in the eyes for a few agitating seconds, and then uttered the words which almost made me burst into hysterical laughter: "Pass along!" He continued to stare, probably to determine the effect on me.

I felt that I was shaking like a leaf, but I must have imagined it. I let my arms fall slowly, bowed, repeated my apology, and—asked if he had a cigarette. "Pass along!"—he literally hissed the words this time and went on to the next man before I had had time to re-mount my bicycle.

The control on the Södal Road did not seem much interested when I rode past with dangerous forebodings, nor did the usual post at Mosby, nor a cyclist patrol I met up among the cliffs. But I breathed a little easier when I reached the hut that evening, especially because everything was still going well there.

The main station in Ovrebö was now working at full capacity, really too vigorously at times, considering the dangerous local situation. There were always more controls, always more strange or mysterious persons reported in the district. The Germans seemed determined to stamp out illegal activities at any price, particularly now when there was no guarantee that the Allies would not attempt a new invasion.

The arrest of many agents in recent weeks had undoubtedly had important results; the Germans were beginning to understand a number of systems which were commonly used and to know the different kinds of equipment, for radio and other Underground activities, which agents were obliged to carry with them from place to place.

As I have said before, we had been well-supplied with food all summer, in spite of being restricted to a monotonous diet while running the reserve station out on Barlindal Moor. But the contacts in Oslo had to have food, as did the stations and contacts in southern Norway.

Nevertheless, we got what we needed—through our contacts upcountry and a contact in Oslo who supplied us with "Danish parcels," or "gifts from the Danish Red Cross to the sick and old." An excellent and most valuable system, one which helped not only us but many others in a similar position.

14 Fresh Supplies

IT WAS TIME NOW to prepare for a new drop of equipment by parachute from the other side. "Pinpoint" had already been fixed for the same area as the earlier drop—the Eiker Forest, north of Darbu Railway Station and northwest of Drammen.

Lars now took over the running of the station, and Jan attended to the most general meteorological observations for the weather reports, so that this should not stop either. I myself took one of the radio sets and two crystals for use in communication between "pinpoint" and London during the period in which the stuff might be dropped.

Before our friend the railway guard left the Oslo-Kristiansand line, he had initiated his successors into the work they were to do for us. The guards who had taken over from him were called Kristian Tveit and Leif Ovesen, and they kept things going to the very end, even under the most difficult conditions. Not only were people to be carried, but there was also to be a regular delivery of messenger mail—and packages.

That everything went as smoothly as it did that season, in spite of constant controls and snoopers

222

among the passengers and at the stations, was due largely to the fine work of these two men.

Kristiansand Railway Station had long ago been put out of bounds for us, so we had to take the local train to Grovane Station and get into the ordinary Sörland train there. The morning I was to go to Oslo, the same thing happened as had happened once before. When the train stopped at Grovane, six German police soldiers and one Norwegian state policeman got off. There had been a control on the stretch from Kristiansand to Grovane.

Tveit, who was standing on the step at the back of the train, nodded cautiously as I went past and got into the next car in front.

We usually traveled to or from Oslo on the night train, because there was less danger of a control on it. But on this occasion I didn't have time to wait. As far as Kongsberg everything was normal, but there the stationmaster volunteered unpleasant news that there was a state of emergency at Vestfossen and Mjöndal; consequently, there was great danger of a thorough examination. No passenger was allowed to get off the train at these two stations, where German patrols had taken up positions with machine guns, and complete fighting equipment.

The train should really have stopped, but this time it went slowly through both stations—by agreement between the engineer and the guard in charge. Passengers for those stations had to take the first train back next morning—but I arrived in Oslo safe and sound without any further setbacks.

In Oslo our head office had been informed of the time of the parachute drop, and all preparations had been made. Four men—the Elligers twins, Morten Hancke, and Botolf Botolfsen—were again sent up. But because of the state of emergency, which had just been canceled, I made a trip up to Darbu for safety's sake to investigate the conditions a little more closely. It would be very unlucky for all of us if we brought down all the things dropped and handed them straight over to the Germans.

Unfortunately, all was not as serene as it might have been, either upcountry or along the roads down to Hakavik. There had been raids on the farms along this blind-alley road, usually so quiet and peaceful; there had been searches at the Hakavik power works which had yielded as booty only a hidden sedan. Nevertheless, according to the farmer at Darbu, a whole gang of "men in green" had spread out into these parts that very day. It was hard to say exactly what was up, but it was rumored that the Germans were after concealed arms and ammunition.

Then I looked up the Mil. Org. driver. I took the train down to Vestfossen, where everything seemed quiet now, and walked for half an hour up to the house where Odvar Nyrud lived. Last time, when we had met in such an odd but lucky manner up at Store Oeksne, we had arranged that he should drive again later if it was convenient. Yes, Nyrud was at home, but a number of changes had taken place since we last saw one another.

He was no longer working for Mastebogen or driving along the road between the Store Oeksne Dam and Vestfossen, and he was no longer driving an ordinary truck, but a timber truck without a deck;

in short, his field of activity was no longer one in which we were interested. This was a serious setback. I have seldom met a man who worked as hard as Nyrud did to find the best solution to a problem, regardless of whether that solution might mean death for him.

On the following Sunday, he told me, he would not be working; he might perhaps be able to "borrow" a truck; if he could, he would come up if we could let him know in advance that the drop had taken place. If not, he thought he could get another man whom he could induce to drive, in spite of the risk.

Once that was arranged, I returned to Oslo, and our further plans were gone through for the last time during the night. Next morning two of us went to Darbu, to our friend the farmer Granbakken and stayed there overnight.

The report from Hakavik was better, but not altogether reassuring. Early the same morning a large German truck had driven past and taken the road to the power works, where the road up to Store Oeksne begins winding up the side of the ridge. The truck had not come back yet, and that meant that we must wait till next day.

At half-past seven in the morning the truck came along with the confiscated sedan in tow. So that was all they were after! It was better than we had dared hope. We went down on our bicycles and looked up another farmer who lived close to the road and had helped us in the past. He was able to tell us a little about the investigations that had been made, but not enough to be of any real help.

Instead of passing Hakavik ourselves, we turned off

from the main road before we got that far. There was
no need to excite people's imaginations; last spring,
when the reception committee, carrying heavy packages, had passed the place on their way to meet us,
rumors had at once begun to circulate, and the watchman at the Store Oeksne Dam had received special
orders to look out for saboteurs.

That night, we slept on the old camping ground
near the dam, and next morning at the appointed
time we opened contact with London. The watch at
"pinpoint" had been postponed one day and would
start on September 27.

Before we went into the woods this time, we had
thoroughly investigated the dam watchman, who
lived a ten-minute walk from the dam itself. He was
evidently O.K., although he seemed astonished when
we laid our cards frankly on the table. We told him we
were waiting for a parachute drop; he would undoubtedly hear the plane when it came. We did not
want any official announcement, only his support in
arranging an efficient warning system.

The watchman was in telephonic communication
with the works down at Hakavik; there was also a
phone at the dam itself. Both telephones were on the
same line; two rings meant the call was for the dam,
one ring meant it was for the watchman's house. Yes,
he told us, he had a very good fellow down at the
works, with whom he had had dealings before.

The arrangement was quite clear: in case any outside persons arrived immediately after the drop, the
man down at the works would phone the dam watchman. We would station one of our men at the watch-

man's, and if a telephone message came our sentry would hurry to "pinpoint" and warn us. Then we could leave all the supplies and equipment in their hiding places and take the road down toward Sandsvaer or the Eidfoss Mills with a head start of at least three-quarters of an hour.

In the course of the evening, Ottomar and Carl arrived, followed around eleven o'clock by Botolf, who brought an unpleasant bit of news: earlier in the evening twelve German soldiers and three officers had come to the Hakavik electric works and demanded quarters. They claimed to be woodcutters, and said they were going to fell some timber for a large German camp near Vestfossen.

This was an awkward situation, if not actually a dangerous one. What did it mean? Germans felling timber for themselves! I had never heard of such a thing before. And why just now? For a moment my thoughts went back to the life-and-death chase over Svaland Moor a year before; we certainly didn't want a repetition of that. Would we be forced to call off the drop altogether, wait for the next favorable period, and move "pinpoint" to some other place?

After all the possibilities had been carefully weighed and discussed, we decided to continue as we had begun. The next day was spent in combing the ground around "pinpoint" to examine the possibility of our being bothered by "tourists." Unfortunately there were two men living in a hut a few hundred yards from where supplies had previously been dropped. This place, therefore, could not be used.

We moved down to a larger stretch of marsh, nearer

to the Oeksne and the dam, to which the stuff would have to be carried away. This spot, too, was not far from the hut where the two linesmen were living while they inspected the power line over to Sandsvaer.

To be on the safe side, we took a little walk in their direction and started a conversation to find out what kind of men they were. I have never seen two fellows more furious than they became when I told them that we belonged to the State Police and asked if they had seen anything of some "students" in those parts. If there hadn't been three of us, I don't think we would have got out of that hut unharmed! Well, they seemed to be all right, so no further steps were necessary.

Carl Elligers really should not have come on this trip, because his injured knee was still giving him trouble. But Carl was one of those fellows who would never be content to stay home if anything special was brewing. This time, too, it had been impossible to keep him away. He was assigned the job of sitting at the dam watchman's to warn us if anything unforeseen happened.

We still remembered vividly how hard it had been to carry all the equipment last time, so this time we arranged for a boat—the watchman's barge, which was supposed to be used only on duty. To protect him, we went through the motions of "stealing" the barge by breaking the lock. And of course it was pure chance that the oars had been hidden where they were easy to find.

On the evening of the twenty-seventh, two of us walked down to the watchman's, as usual, to contact London and find out whether anything was going to happen. As soon as the watchman appeared at the door we could see that something was wrong. Two German noncommissioned officers had been in only twenty minutes earlier.

This was disturbing—had one of our own people talked? But who on earth could it have been? Did the Germans have full information about what was going to happen?

It was time now to make contact. While the dam watchman was sitting on the steps outside having a smoke, a message came over the radio: "We are coming tonight!" Things began to move; the radio set was securely packed and hidden in a particular spot behind the watchman's house Carl stayed there while I went up to the dam, took the boat, and rowed three-quarters of the way up to the northwest end of Store Oeksne. From there it was only a fifteen-minute walk to the camp at "pinpoint."

Everything was packed up; only the tent was left standing so that we might have something to creep into while we waited. Screened lights were readied, and from 11:15 P.M. we kept watch.

It was brilliant weather, starry and cold with a light northerly breeze. The moon was just about to creep up over the ridges to eastward; things couldn't have been more ideal if they had been especially ordered for a successful operation. Time crept by. Now and then we sprang up, hearing the noise of planes. But it was only a false alarm; the noise came from far away to the south—a big raid somewhere. We sank back into the heather, where we huddled behind a large boulder the better to keep warm.

It was 12:40 A.M. Then came the noise of a plane again, this time from the southwest, and soon the silhouette of a Halifax appeared, faint against the starry sky. It drew nearer—there was no doubt that it was ours. Light! I sent the call sign, a series of *D*'s. The plane passed over "pinpoint," swung farther north, and came in at a lower altitude straight toward the marsh where we stood ready.

Then, suddenly, several hundred yards before it got right over us, it swung out to the side and dropped sharply to a lower altitude. I stopped flashing. The plane passed—and seven parachutes opened up, one after another, silhouetted against the full moon!

Here was trouble—the parachutes were at least a mile and a quarter from where we stood. What in the world had happened? We stood staring hard at the parachutes to fix the direction accurately in our minds, till they disappeared into the darkness and among the trees. Then we started running.

We searched for an hour in the depths of the woods before we found all the containers; every single parachute was entangled in the treetops. It was after five in the morning before everything was more or less unpacked. The parachute harness was distributed in various hiding places; some of the containers were sunk in a small pond, others were covered up where they lay.

However bad the drop may have been, it had one advantage. The way down to the Oeksne, where the boat lay ready, had been shortened by a mile and a quarter, so there would be only five hundred yards of carrying when we began moving the supplies. But we still wondered—why had the pilot so suddenly altered course and then dropped the containers anyway?

I did not learn the answer until months later, when I met the pilot in a London club. He told me that as he was coming in for the drop, he had suddenly seen a light turned on about a mile and a quarter beyond "pinpoint." He assumed that tourists were there, and was determined that they should not see much of the performance, although he fully realized that the whole plan might fail because of the sudden change in "pinpoint." A slightly stronger wind could have sent the whole cargo down into the Oeksne. The light he had seen could have come only from the hut where the two linesmen were staying.

After we had hidden everything, the others crept into their bags while I took the first watch. It had become light, the sky had clouded over a good deal, and it looked as if we would have rain. Well, there could be nothing better.

For the present all was quiet, and there was little danger of any visitors before the day was well advanced. It would take the Germans considerable time to come up from Hakavik, and it would be difficult for them to find out approximately where the drop had been made, if anyone had suspected it. All we could do was wait and see what happened, and hope that we would not have a visit from Carl before the time fixed.

The whole day passed without anything unusual happening. Carl came up at 6:00 P.M. as arranged, and could only report that all was well. We began to move the containers, one by one, down to where the boat lay well camouflaged with boughs. About eight in the evening we sighted a Storch overhead, but it disappeared northward after flying back and forth over the Eiker.

On Saturday, September 30, everything was still peaceful. Botolf was now sent to Oslo to arrange things in town and get everything ready for receiving the supplies. Ottomar was sent down to Darbu for cardboard boxes which were being sent there meantime from Oslo. At the same time he would look in on Nyrud and find out whether he could drive as agreed.

Ottomar came back that afternoon with good news that all was quiet in the valley and that Nyrud had arranged to get another truck and would be at the dam as agreed at twelve o'clock Sunday—the next day.

At 9:30 A.M., three men went aboard the fully loaded barge. We were barely able to stay afloat, although the barge was unusually large and solid. It was pitch-dark as, with a fresh breeze behind us, we rowed the entire cargo to the dam in three-quarters of an hour.

Not a sound was heard apart from the sighing of the wind and the splashing of the water. A light rain was falling. One after another the containers were moved into the boathouse, the contents repacked in cardboard boxes, and the containers taken out in the barge and sunk.

We worked until midnight, packing and closing the boxes and labeling them WITH CARE—GLASS! Finally we lay down, exhausted, in the sawdust under the floor of the sawmills; if anyone came, the dam watchman had promised to let us know as soon as he received a warning from below by telephone. It was very cold; the thermometer registered four degrees below freezing.

At 5:00 A.M. we were at it again, packing boxes. We

had posted a sentry now, to be on the safe side. All was still quiet, and remained so till ten minutes to eleven, when there was sudden excitement: the dam watchman came up on his bicycle, puffing and blowing, and told us that a German had phoned from the power works and asked if he had seen anything of two soldiers who had disappeared while at work and were presumed to have deserted.

The dam watchman was strongly of the opinion that the Germans would come up to look for the deserters. Our view was that their real reason for telephoning was an entirely different one, and that the story about the "deserters" was only a pretext. The watchman was convinced that something was radically wrong; he vanished downhill on his bicycle like greased lightning, after receiving exact instructions on how to act if and when the Germans arrived at the dam.

Practically everything was now repacked in cardboard boxes, ten large and six smaller ones, plus three paper bags containing parachutes. We worked till the sweat streamed down us, to remove all outward traces.

Not more than five minutes after the watchman had vanished downhill, the sentry reported a horse and cart on the road to the dam. More people were coming. The doors of the boathouse were shut in an instant; Ottomar and Carl disappeared across the dam and up the slope on the other side; I remained seated on the planks down by the sawmills. The man in the cart turned out to be one of the peasants from the valley; he was coming up to get some fir planks with which to build a boat.

To avoid suspicion and get rid of him as quickly as possible, I helped the man load the planks in his cart.

But the fellow seemed to have time to spare! I couldn't very well drive him away, or tell him that we had the contents of a parachute drop hidden in the shed, waiting to be collected at twelve o'clock.

He talked and talked, made me smoke a pipe of homemade tobacco, held forth about conditions here and there. At last—at five minutes to twelve—he turned his horse and started off. But the load was so heavy that the horse could not pull it up the short slope above the dam. The man had to unload half of it, take the cart over the crucial point, and then carry one plank at a time up to where it now stood.

Naturally, he was astonished at the energetic help I gave him, and he was perhaps even more astonished at the unfriendly tone I had assumed. But he was such a simple fellow that he didn't suspect anything even when I practically told him to clear out!

Morten was now sent down to Darbu, partly to reduce our numbers at the dam in case anything should happen, and partly because we were anxious to get him to Oslo as quickly as possible. He was to arrange for the transport by truck of all the stuff that had been sent to Skarpsno and Skøyen railway stations. Ottomar, Carl, and I continued to await developments up on the hillside.

Not many minutes had passed after the peasant's departure when we caught the sound of a car on its way up the rocky ascent to the dam, where we sat holding our Sten guns. Now the important question: Were the Germans coming to look for "deserters," or was it Odvar Nyrud, our own truck driver?

An ordinary Norwegian motor truck with a generator came in sight at the bend; it must be Odvar. As a precaution Ottomar and Carl continued sitting where they were, while I sauntered down, happy to be able to give the signal a moment later that it was Odvar. But the news he brought gave us something to worry about: on the road from Vestfossen to Hakavik he had driven past two closed German cars, and on the road into the power works he had seen several Germans standing talking together.

There was no doubt that something was up. Should we take the chance? Was Nyrud willing to drive—to have a try?

As usual, the fellow could not refuse, but he asked us to let him have a gun, in case he needed it. The cardboard boxes were hoisted on to the deck of the truck in a few minutes; all the time we were expecting to hear the telephone at the dam ring twice, the signal we had agreed on. But nothing happened—for the time being.

Everything was ready at last. Ottomar and Carl took their sacks and went off across the dam and up the ridge on the other side. The plan was for them to take the "back way" down to the village, where they had hidden their bicycles, then ride to Drammen and take the train from there. Thus there were only two of us in the truck: Odvar Nyrud and myself. In case things went wrong and I had not reached Oslo the same evening, everyone was to go into hiding and await developments.

We started, with our revolvers on our knees. But we had gone scarcely fifty yards when Nyrud stopped abruptly, and at the same time we both jumped in our seats: a motorcycle and sidecar, with two German police soldiers and an officer, swung over the brow of the hill and braked sharply.

"Shoot!" whispered Nyrud. "Let's get them!"

"No, hold on a moment—don't shoot till I tell you! There are sure to be more of them farther down!"

The officer in the sidecar had risen with one hand on his revolver holster and the other in the air. "Halt!" he shouted.

I opened the door and got halfway out onto the step; with one hand I kept a tight hold of the revolver, which was hidden by the front of the truck. The German on the pillion carried a machine gun and had only to pull the trigger if we offered any opposition.

"Back a little, so as to get them alongside us!" I whispered.

Nyrud backed with one hand on the wheel; he had his revolver in the other. The word bloodthirsty does not adequately describe his expression.

"Come up alongside!" I called to the Germans, beckoning to them. They came slowly, with the officer still standing up in the sidecar.

"Halt, and stop your engine!" He repeated his order in German, a language which we, of course, did not understand at all.

"Shall I step on the gas?" Nyrud asked in a low voice. I had no time to answer; he was leaning out toward the Germans, who had now stopped beside us, while the officer was looking with interest at the large covered pile of cardboard boxes in the truck.

"Stop the engine!" he commanded.

"Wait till they've stopped their own engine!" I whispered to Odvar. He waited. At the same moment, the officer got out of the sidecar and the driver of the motorcycle closed his throttle and turned off the ignition.

"*Now!*" Odvar had long before changed over from generator to gasoline, and he "stepped on the gas" in the fullest sense of the world! What actually happened I still find it hard to understand, but we were around the bend before the first shot was fired. We both sat automatically huddled up in the driver's seat, expecting a charge from behind at any moment. But it did not come!

How we drove! Not for nothing had Nyrud driven along this stretch of narrow stony forest road to Hakavik for several years with heavy loads of timber and planks; he knew every bend and every boulder. He still kept a tight hold of his revolver. We slid around one bend after another at breakneck speed; every moment I expected the limb of a fir tree to come crashing into the driver's cab.

I kept looking first ahead and then behind. Suddenly, as we slid around a sharp bend and bumped over a large stone at the same time, one of the paper bags tumbled off the deck. Was it one of the parachute bags?

"Go on down and try to push through!" I shouted to Odvar. "If it gets too hot, you'll have to stop and run into the woods; I'll clear the bag out of the way and try to hold the Germans up for a few minutes, to give you a longer start. We must warn Ottomar and Carl!"

Odvar slowed down a little to let me jump off, and in a few seconds the truck had disappeared around the next bend; I ran back and cleared the paper bag out of the way, scrambled up the slope at the side of the road, and lay down. Not a sound was to be

heard. What had happened to the Germans—had their
motorcycle broken down? Or had they stopped chasing
us because they knew there were more Germans
farther down, ready to capture the truck?

I lay waiting for a quarter of an hour. All remained
quiet. But Ottomar and Carl were on their way down
with many things in their sacks which would be fatal
evidence against them if they came up against a control. I went down across the valley and up on the other
side as fast as I could; if I could reach the path where
it approached the main road before the boys got that
far, I could stop them in time.

I arrived out of breath, threw myself down behind a
fir, and waited. Ten minutes passed, and I cautiously
drew back under cover; someone was coming from
above. It was Ottomar and Carl, whistling and singing,
without a notion of what had happened to us. The
sacks were emptied of everything that had to do with
the job, and the twins went on down to carry out the
original plan.

I myself took the road back to the dam, chiefly to
retrieve my sack, which was still lying up there with all
the most important papers, well hidden under the root
of a tree on the west side of the dam.

When I got there, all was comparatively quiet; there
was not a sign of the motorcycle. Perhaps it was lying
somewhere lower down along the forest track after
having tried to catch up with Nyrud. I took my sack
and set off downhill, gathered up all the things that
had been removed from Ottomar's and Carl's sacks,
and continued down to where the bicycle lay hidden.

For an hour I remained concealed behind a tree
with a good view of the road. Five German cars had

passed. Yes, there was something happening somewhere! But what was it? It would be reckless to run
the risk of a control with that sack; so without luggage,
and without anything which had any connection with
illegal work, I got on the bicycle and rode off toward
Darbu. Three German cars passed, but not one displayed any interest in me. They were all traveling at
high speed.

It could only be Nyrud, I decided, who had caused
all this activity; in any case, it was impossible at the
moment to find any other explanation. I received an
entirely different explanation, however, from a contact
along the road.

There was then a "celebrity" nicknamed Rottenikken
in the Norwegian criminal world, and the whole thing
was his fault from start to finish. He had murdered the
sheriff's officer at Sem, kidnaped his wife, plundered
a number of houses, and taken to the woods in a wild,
desperate flight.

He had last been seen in the neighborhood of the
Hakavik works, and it was generally believed that he
had taken the road up toward the Oeksne and the
country behind it. Thirty Norwegian State Police and
more than twenty Germans had gone in to search for
him.

The farmer was also able to tell me that a motor
truck belonging to a firm at Vestfossen had come at
breakneck speed down the road from the Oeksne Dam,
and that two men in the driver's seat had fired at random when German policemen had tried to stop the
truck, both by the dam watchman's cabin and down at
the crossroads where the forest road runs into the main
road to Darbu and Vestfossen.

After that the driver had gone right over a tree with which the Germans had tried to block the road, had run over at least three Germans and shot another, got through, and continued along the road toward Vestfossen. The farmer told me that he himself had stood and watched the truck rush past with two German cars just behind it, the Germans firing as hard as they could during the chase. What had happened afterward he did not know; but it was believed that Rottenikken had had some accomplice, or that he had forced the driver to help him escape.

I could tell from the farmer's manner of speech and his excitement that the story was exaggerated, although much of it was true. What had happened later? I wondered.

The road became quieter; just a man or two walked quickly past. I went on to the crossroads, and along the same road back to the spot where I had hidden the package. Not a car was to be seen on the way back. At about eight o'clock I decided to risk going on, and strange to say, I got all the way to Darbu without being stopped. Every time a car or motorcycle came along I laid my bicycle down in the ditch and skipped into the woods.

I walked over to the platform of the Darbu Railway Station, and nearly fell flat when I saw all the cardboard boxes stacked along the wall of the baggage room with a large tarpaulin over them! So Nyrud had brought it off! Or had the Germans themselves placed them there after capturing Nyrud? And were they just waiting for someone to come and claim them?

I retreated cautiously into the waiting room with a

feeling all the time that fifty pairs of eyes were following my every movement. But no, it was just my imagination. The ticket agent, who was one of our people, told me that the truck had brought it off by "taking a few short cuts" over a field or two and along some farm tracks before getting back to the main road.

All the cardboard boxes were now to be sent to Oslo in pairs, as baggage, each pair by a different train on the first five days. The plan had to be changed somewhat, however, because a large quantity of dynamite and explosives had been stolen at Hönefoss. There was a state of emergency there, and a number of railway stations, as well as the freight office in Oslo, were being systematically searched. All our packages were sent by three different trains to Sköyen, where they were picked up by truck and driven to 8 Nils Juelsgate for distribution!

What had happened to Odvar Nyrud? We hesitated to make direct inquiries at his home, for fear of walking straight into the hands of the Gestapo. But the incident was almost certain to result in trouble for Nyrud; the truck he had used had the firm's name on its side; it would be the easiest thing in the world to find out who had driven it.

But Odvar had vanished; no one knew where he had gone. We assumed that he had made his way to a training camp which Mil. Org. maintained somewhere upcountry.

One would have to search for a long time before he could find another driver like Odvar Nyrud.

15 Now We Go to England

ONE DAY WE RECEIVED an urgent message telling us that the Germans had begun to set up a permanent direction-finding station inside the German camp close by. That was the proverbial last straw!

During the preceding week we had not been able to obtain reports from our German informers, evidently because the investigations down in the port were being steadily intensified. In view of the conditions under which the station was now operating, as well as the beginning of seasonal bad weather which hindered air operations, it was decided to close the station and our entire activities in southern Norway.

The way the situation in Europe had developed since the Allied invasion, it was only a question of how long the Germans could hold out. As to Norway, there was still no way of knowing whether there would be open warfare.

Lars was the first to leave. He paid a lightning visit to town, where he was able to meet his family at the home of some acquaintances. It was a big risk to take, but it ended happily in spite of controls both coming and going. Then he was off to Oslo.

Jan and I remained a few days to pack. Some things

were put into watertight cans and hidden in the woods; the more essential pieces of equipment were packed in cardboard boxes and prepared for shipment to Oslo by train. Gunnar Upsahl undertook to arrange for them to be sent off, and he did not fail us.

Jan took with him all the meteorological equipment and a quantity of weapons. He narrowly escaped falling into the hands of a German patrol down among the rocks and again at Mosby Station. Luckily, he evaded them and took the local train to Grovane; from there he went to Oslo via the Sörland Railway, accompanied by our friend Leif Ovesen.

I had to go into Kristiansand and arrange matters with our associates there, in case anything should happen after we had left. Our German friends were the greatest problem. They were now determined to steal the police boat and go across the North Sea to England—the old plan which we had thus far headed off.

The plan was now, if anything, more crackbrained than ever. In the first place, the weather would make such a voyage impossible in a half-decked craft which was not built for a rough sea. Secondly, they would most certainly never get out of the harbor without being caught, as they had no knowledge of seamanship and knew nothing about boats of that type.

To us there was a far more important reason why they should not leave their post now. We were counting on continued contact between Sven Nordahl-Hansen and these two, based on a system of messengers eastward into Sweden. It was not impossible that we might later be forced to return to the same district if, contrary to expectation, the war should drag on for a long time.

Further, if these two cleared out now Sven would be compelled to go into hiding, as it was already common knowledge that the three had been on good terms. This would cause a serious break in the whole system down in Kristiansand. If Sven did not clear out, he would undoubtedly be arrested if the two Germans disappeared. On the other hand, if the Germans were arrested there would still be a possibility of keeping Sven as a liaison.

After some negotiation and discussion, the Germans agreed to remain in their jobs, and the contemplated voyage across the North Sea was indefinitely postponed. Sven, too, continued in his job. These arrangements would have settled things satisfactorily, if other complications had not cropped up immediately.

I went back to Mosby, where the sack with all the most important equipment and the suitcase containing the American radio transmitter had been placed in the cloakroom. From there I took the local to Grovane, where I jumped aboard the ordinary night train to Oslo. Tveit was acting as guard, and that simplified matters.

When we reached Kongsberg, we learned that a state of emergency had been declared at Hokksund. Nobody knew exactly why. Tveit made his own arrangements for the sack with our supplies, while I took the suitcase containing the American transmitter and sat down in the corridor of a third-class car. The train was overcrowded as usual, so I stood the suitcase on end in the corridor, laid my raincoat over it, and sat on top of it all.

"Hokksund!" The train ran slowly into the station. There were Germans everywhere, ordinary soldiers and police soldiers. No passengers were permitted to get out; even the train guard was not allowed to enter the station buildings. There was a rapid search of each car, and samples were taken from people's luggage. In fact, it looked as if the Germans were more interested in the appearance of the luggage on the racks than in the people themselves.

Of course passports and tickets were examined, but as far as I could see no interest was shown in travel permits. To me, sitting on top of the American radio transmitter, the situation was nerve-racking; but nobody showed the slightest interest in anything about me except my passport, and it was in perfect order. That was all—for the time being, at least—and the train was given permission to proceed.

In Oslo things were in pretty good order, at any rate as far as we were concerned. A number of arrests and raids had set people's imaginations working, and one could never be sure what were facts and what were fancies. People of all classes were in hiding, waiting for a chance to get over into Sweden; the export organizations were operating at high pressure—that is, those that were still operating at all. The atmosphere generally was far from pleasant.

Within a week all our packages arrived from Mosby, thanks to Gunnar, who did an excellent job as usual. But getting the things from the station to the places to which they were addressed was no longer a simple matter; and here, once more, the women did a wonderful job. The stuff was repacked, arms separately, radio

parts and transmitters separately, clothes and other
things in a simpler way.

Again we played hide-and-seek through the streets
of Oslo to get the things deposited in the various
dumps outside the town. At Muren in Baerum, Larsen
and his wife were again willing to receive anything of
any kind, despite a recent raid on their farm. The Germans had turned everything upside down in the farm-
house and barn; little did their leader guess, when he
stood on top of a pile of bricks outside the police hut,
that under the bricks lay a whole load of things that
would not bear being brought to light!

Kaare and Ingeborg Larsen did not work only for us.
At regular intervals, prisoners from Grini on outside
work came in with their guards and got as much food,
tobacco, and other things as they wanted. Down at
Bekkestua there was a Nazi with the same name, Kaare
Larsen, and to be on the safe side the National Socialists sent pamphlets to them both! In this way Kaare
and Ingeborg were among our best contacts outside
Oslo.

We pushed ahead with the work in Oslo for more
than a fortnight, till everything was settled. Lars was
sent to Sweden, arriving there safely after an exhaust-
ing journey. Conditions along the frontier were not as
good as they had been; considerable snow had fallen,
and the guides on the different routes were uneasy
because of the tracks, which told their own story.

Jan and I started out together on what proved to be
a tough journey. It took us a week to reach a point that
was three hours from the actual frontier. The party we
were in consisted of four men, not counting the guide.
But another party which had started an hour earlier on

the same route had come up against German patrols; two men had been shot, the other two had been pursued a long way into Swedish territory.

The guide who met us and reported this incident refused to make the last part of the journey; it was hopeless to try to get through, as the Germans had set up machine-gun posts every hundred yards between the two lakes where we were to cross. Two hours from our goal, and we had to turn back! It was a bitter decision, but the guide clearly knew what he was talking about. Back we went the way we had come —all the way back to Skarnes.

There were controls and guard posts everywhere, and the motor drive from the bridge at Skarnes down to Eidsvoll will never be forgotten by anyone who took part in it.

We set off again, and at last we were in Sweden— after covering more than a hundred miles in deep snow in four days, walking openly through Austmarka by night and day on a sparkling, crackling crust of snow— to cross, at last, that street cut through the countryside which marks the frontier.

The nightmare was over! At last one could go about as his real self, instead of skulking about like a homeless gypsy or a hunted beast. To be sure, I still had one hurdle to take in the shape of the detective-inspector in the Swedish magistrate's office, who declared that he had seen me once before under another name; but that difficulty was quickly straightened out when I convinced the authorities that it must have been a cousin of mine who looked incredibly like me, and had been taken for my twin brother from childhood.

The name was the same and the other data agreed

with what I was able to tell them, so inquiries by telephone to the police in Gothenburg produced nothing
to contradict my statements. Whether the detective-
inspector was satisfied with my explanation is another
matter. Ironically, he was thrown into jail himself
three weeks later, charged with espionage on behalf
of a foreign power!

We stayed in Stockholm for three weeks. There were
reports to be written and a lot of work to be done in
connection with future action at home. Lars, Jan, and
I often sat studying developments at home since we
had left Oslo. Messages streamed into the office in
Stockholm, telling us that conditions were becoming
more and more difficult. At Stavanger, one of our best
agents had been arrested along with a number of his
contacts.

And then came the news that shook us more than
anything else had so far. It came at the same time in
two telegrams, one from the Swedish Legation in Oslo,
the other from one of our contacts there: "Carl Sigurd
Elligers shot in raid at 8 Nils Juelsgate 23rd. Ottomar
Elligers, Sven Nordahl-Hansen, and Otto arrested same
place. Leif Paulsen arrested Kristiansand."

So it had happened! One of my best comrades, a
friend from early childhood, from the life in forest and
field as Scouts, from the years during the war, in
which he had worked untiringly for the Norwegian
cause, for the land he loved so deeply. Once more, it
was the best among us who had made the supreme
sacrifice.

What had happened? Months were to pass before we
heard the details. Connections we had been forced to

break with had continued to work for another Underground organization. It was the same old story of a file which the possessor was compelled to betray after torture. A man who at times had obtained passport photographs for us for some reason had decided to keep a copy for himself. He had also had dealings by messenger with the Elligers twins in Oslo.

In his file, which was found by the Gestapo, was a piece of paper with the notation: "O. C. Elligers, 8 Nils Juelsgate, Oslo."

He had left the file with another man; he himself managed to escape.

From Stockholm Jan and I went on together by air to London. There our ways parted; Jan met his fiancée, whom he had not seen for more than five years. They were married within a fortnight, and I had the honor of being best man at their wedding three hours before leaving for Canada.

Lars came over a week later, to acquire fresh knowledge in the branch in which he was now serving. Two months later he was dropped into Norway, and continued doing splendid work there till the liberation came.

On May 8, 1945, the peace bells rang; for most it was a message of joy, for some of sorrow—they had lost. None of us will ever forget that day. We had won! Six long years of privation and misery were ended at last.

A short time afterward I flew in over Norwegian mountains, and along the Norwegian coast which was bathed in summer sunshine. There lay the land we had fought for, free and lovelier than ever before; the land for which Norwegians throughout the centuries had sacrificed everything. It was again our own! That was our victory—but it was dearly bought.

We gathered again to celebrate victory—Rolf Millang, Hjelm Basberg, Jan Tenvig, Ottomar Elligers, Lars Larsen, and all the others who had given so much; connections, too, who had been sent to Germany or been held in Norwegian prisons; men and women who had served valiantly all through those years.

Only one of us was missing: Carl Sigurd Elligers, one of the thousands who had sacrificed all for Norway—and for freedom.